BUILDING
Vocabulary
Skills

Level K
Student Edition

Columbus, OH • Chicago, IL • Redmond, WA

The McGraw·Hill Companies

www.sra4kids.com

McGraw-Hill SRA

Send all inquiries to:
SRA/McGraw-Hill
8787 Orion Place
Columbus, OH 43240-4027

Printed in the United States of America.

ISBN 0-07-579611-2

4 5 6 7 8 9 QPD 07 06 05 04

Table of Contents

Unit 1

Lesson 1: "School" Vocabulary 2

Word Meanings: What Do You Know?

Reference Skills: Picture Definitions

Build New Vocabulary: Word Relationships

Word Play: Words That Sound Alike

Lesson 2: Our Classroom 6

Word Meanings: Categorization

Reference Skills: Classroom Labeling

Build New Vocabulary: Adding *–s*

Word Play: Color Words

Lesson 3: Playground Vocabulary 10

Word Meanings: Examples

Reference Skills: Multiple Meanings

Build New Vocabulary: Action Words

Word Play: Rhyming Words

Lesson 4: Question Words 14

Word Meanings: Using Question Words

Reference Skills: Word Wall

Build New Vocabulary: Word Web

Word Play: Question Games

Lesson 5: Vocabulary for Places 18

Word Meanings: Descriptions

Reference Skills: Picture Dictionary

Build New Vocabulary: People and Places

Word Play: Silly Sentences

Lesson 6: Vocabulary Review 22

Review Word Meanings: What We Do at School

Unit 2

Lesson 7: "Shadows" Vocabulary 26

Word Meanings: Listening for Meaning

Reference Skills: Synonyms

Build New Vocabulary: Opposites

Word Play: Tongue Twisters

Lesson 8: "Directions" Vocabulary 30

Word Meanings: Opposites Attract

Reference Skills: Word Wall

Build New Vocabulary: Giving Directions

Word Play: Silly Rhymes

Lesson 9: Vocabulary for Seasons 34

Word Meanings: Categorization

Reference Skills: A Season Circle

Build New Vocabulary: Words of the Season

Word Play: Word Families

Lesson 10: "Time Words" Vocabulary 38

Word Meanings: Using What I Know

Reference Skills: Alphabetical Order

Build New Vocabulary: How Often Does It Happen?

Word Play: Before and After

Lesson 11: Calendar Vocabulary 42

Word Meanings: Learning Calendar Words

Reference Skills: Marking a Calendar

Build New Vocabulary: Root Words

Word Play: Happy Birthday!

Lesson 12: Vocabulary Review 46

Review Word Meanings: Shadows Throughout the Seasons

Unit 3

Lesson 13: "Finding Friends" Vocabulary 50
- Word Meanings: Showing Meanings
- Reference Skills: Alphabetical Order
- Build New Vocabulary: The Best of *–est*
- Word Play: Describing Best Friends

Lesson 14: Vocabulary About Me 54
- Word Meanings: Reading a Friendly Letter
- Reference Skills: Thesaurus Rex
- Build New Vocabulary: Feelings
- Word Play: Write a Friendly Letter

Lesson 15: Vocabulary for Home 58
- Word Meanings: Compare and Contrast
- Reference Skills: Picture Dictionary
- Build New Vocabulary: Compound Words
- Word Play: What's in My Home?

Lesson 16: "My Day" Vocabulary 62
- Word Meanings: What I Did Today
- Reference Skills: Which Is Correct?
- Build New Vocabulary: Favorite Foods
- Word Play: When Does It Happen?

Lesson 17: Size and Shape 66
- Word Meanings: Identifying Examples
- Reference Skills: Same and Opposite
- Build New Vocabulary: Shapes That Describe
- Word Play: How Does the Story Change?

Lesson 18: Vocabulary Review 70
- Review Word Meanings: Going to the Zoo

Unit 4

Lesson 19: "Wind" Vocabulary 74
- Word Meanings: Venn Diagram
- Reference Skills: Alphabetical Order
- Build New Vocabulary: Adding *-y*
- Word Play: Describing the Weather

Lesson 20: "Stick to It" Vocabulary 78
- Word Meanings: Learn by Doing
- Reference Skills: Which Word Works?
- Build New Vocabulary: Word Relationships
- Word Play: I Can Do It!

Lesson 21: Sound Vocabulary 82
- Word Meanings: Make a Noise!
- Reference Skills: Picture Dictionary
- Build New Vocabulary: More Sound Words
- Word Play: Making Sounds

Lesson 22: "Show and Tell" Vocabulary 86
- Word Meanings: Describing What You See
- Reference Skills: Alphabetical Order
- Build New Vocabulary: Open and Close
- Word Play: I Spy . . .

Lesson 23: Vocabulary for Touch 90
- Word Meanings: Feel the Opposites
- Reference Skills: Cold–Cool–Warm–Hot
- Build New Vocabulary: Sticky, Prickly, Squishy
- Word Play: You're Getting Warmer . . .

Lesson 24: Vocabulary Review 94
- Review Word Meanings: The Windy Race

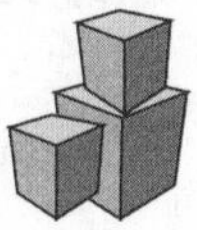

Unit 5

Lesson 25: "Red, White, and Blue" Vocabulary 98
- Word Meanings: Patriotic Meanings
- Reference Skills: Picture Dictionary
- Build New Vocabulary: Proper Nouns
- Word Play: World Neighbors

Lesson 26: "Teamwork" Vocabulary 102
- Word Meanings: Human Knot
- Reference Skills: Body Language
- Build New Vocabulary: Groups
- Word Play: Teamwork

Lesson 27: Compound Words 106
- Word Meanings: Two Animals or One?
- Reference Skills: Picture Equations
- Build New Vocabulary: More Compound Words
- Word Play: Silly Words

Lesson 28: "Make It—Fix It" Vocabulary 110
- Word Meanings: Word Relationships
- Reference Skills: Glue: Noun or Verb?
- Build New Vocabulary: Word Association: Tools
- Word Play: How Do You Make . . . ?

Lesson 29: "Jobs" Vocabulary 114
- Word Meanings: Picture Clues
- Reference Skills: The Suffix *-er*
- Build New Vocabulary: Word Webs
- Word Play: When I Grow Up . . .

Lesson 30: Vocabulary Review 118
- Review Word Meanings: Living and Working in America

Unit 6

Lesson 31: "By the Sea" Vocabulary 122
- Word Meanings: By Land and By Sea
- Reference Skills: Alphabetical Order
- Build New Vocabulary: Sail Away!
- Word Play: The Little Ship That Could

Lesson 32: "Sound Alike" Vocabulary . 126
- Word Meanings: Sound Alike, Look Different
- Reference Skills: Which Is It?
- Build New Vocabulary: Homophones: Words That Sound Alike
- Word Play: Silly Sentences

Lesson 33: Vocabulary for Nature 130
- Word Meanings: Examples/Nonexamples
- Reference Skills: Picture Dictionary
- Build New Vocabulary: Different Kinds of Things
- Word Play: Favorite Nature Place

Lesson 34: "Action Words" Vocabulary 134
- Word Meanings: Show the Action
- Reference Skills: Action Words vs. Nonaction Words
- Build New Vocabulary: More Action Words
- Word Play: Action Charades

Lesson 35: Vocabulary for Cars 138
- Word Meanings: Complete the Sentence
- Reference Skills: Using a Dictionary
- Build New Vocabulary: More Than One Meaning
- Word Play: Same Letter Sounds

Lesson 36: Vocabulary Review 142
- Review Word Meanings: The Scavenger Hunt

Cumulative Review 146

Strategies

Word Webs 150
Categorization 151
Linear Graphs 152
Context Clues 153
Word Relationships 155

Tools and Reference

Table of Contents .... T&R1
Words in Another Country .... T&R2
Prefixes and Suffixes .... T&R3
Base Words .... T&R4
Dolch Words .... T&R5
Fun With Words .... T&R6
Dictionary Skills .... T&R7
Nouns, Verbs, and Adjectives .... T&R9
Glossary .... T&R10
Word Bank .... T&R29

"School" Vocabulary

1 Word Meanings

What Do You Know?

1. read

2. write

3. teacher

ABC

4. think

2+3

5. draw

Score ______
(Top Score 5)

Teacher Read each word aloud. Tell students to draw a circle around the picture that best matches the word.

Vocabulary List

1. teacher
2. student
3. read
4. know
5. quiet
6. classroom
7. right
8. write
9. draw
10. think

2 Reference Skills

Picture Definitions

1. quiet
   draw

2. classroom
   read

3. student
   teacher

4. right
   draw

5. think
   write

2+3

Teacher Read aloud the two words beside each picture definition. Tell students to draw a circle around the word that matches the picture.

Score ______
(Top Score 5)

3 Build New Vocabulary

Word Relationships

1. write

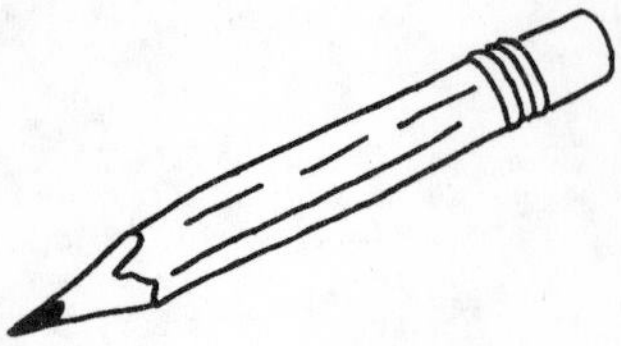

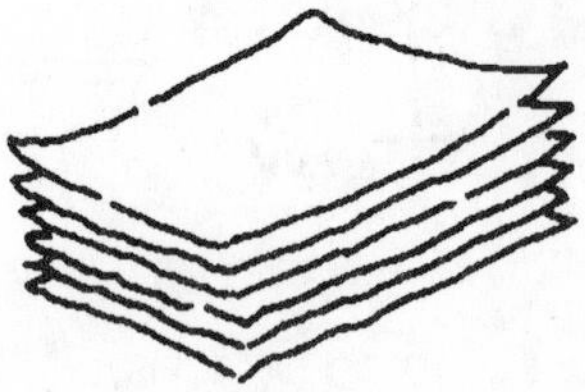

2. draw

3. read

Three
Little
Pigs

4. teacher

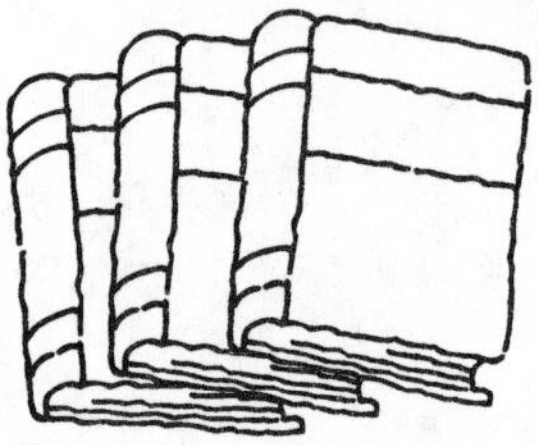

5. quiet

Score ______
(Top Score 5)

Teacher Read each word aloud. Tell students to draw an X over the picture that does NOT relate to the word.

Vocabulary List
1. teacher
2. student
3. read
4. know
5. quiet
6. classroom
7. right
8. write
9. draw
10. think

4 Word Play

Words That Sound Alike

1. Lucy knows the answer.

2. Dad yelled, "No!" at the cat.

3. Matteo writes the letters of the alphabet.

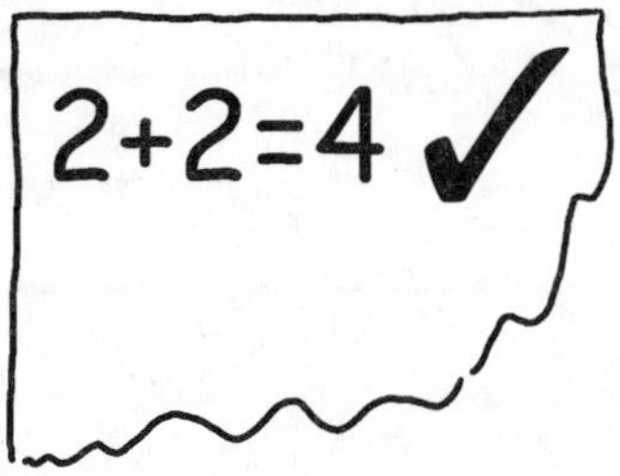
2+2=4 ✓

4. You got the right answer!

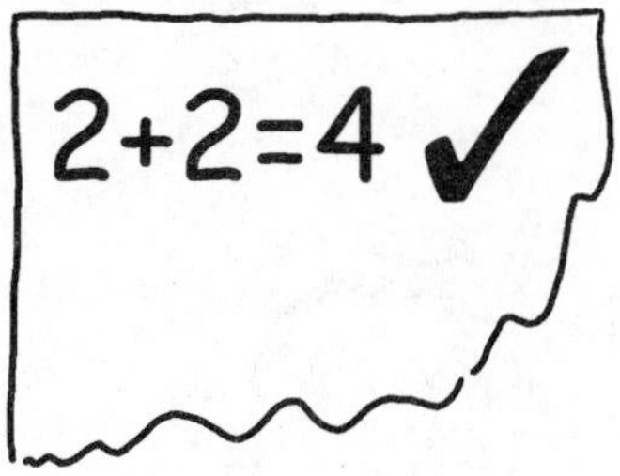
2+2=4 ✓

Teacher Read each sentence aloud. Tell students to circle the picture that matches the underlined word.

Score ______
(Top Score 4)

Our Classroom

1 Word Meanings

Categorization

1.

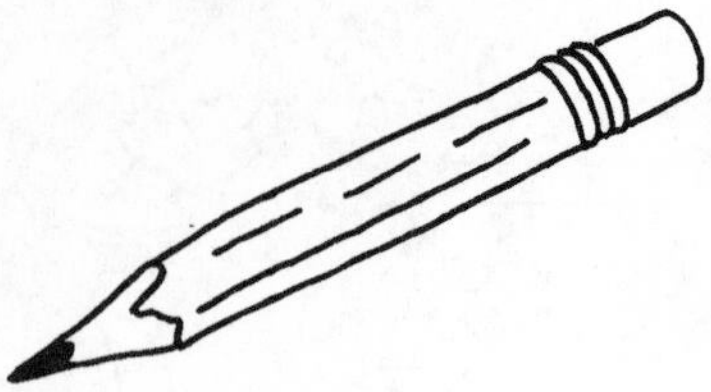

2.

Three
Little
Pigs

GLUE

DAILY NEWS

3.

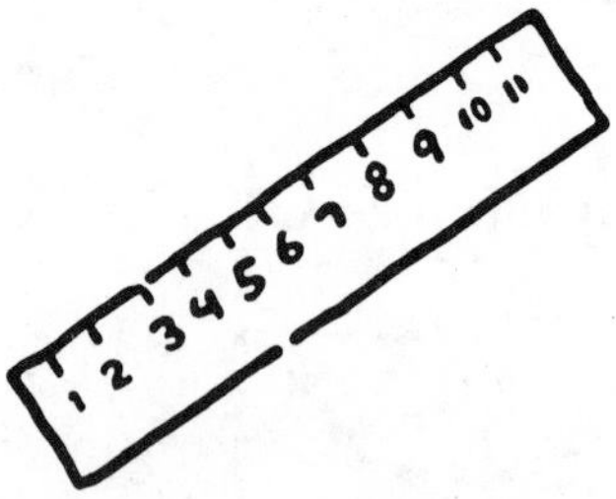
1 2 3 4 5 6 7 8 9 10 11
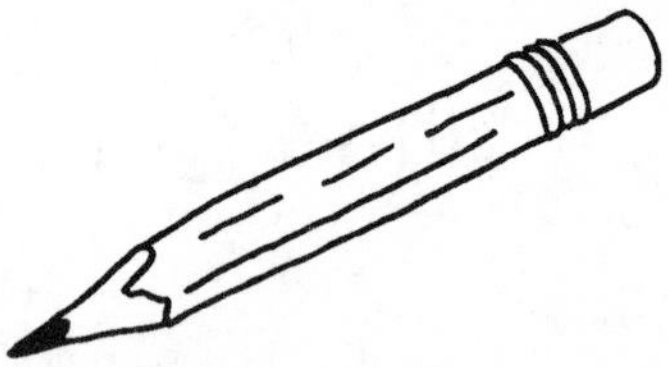

4.

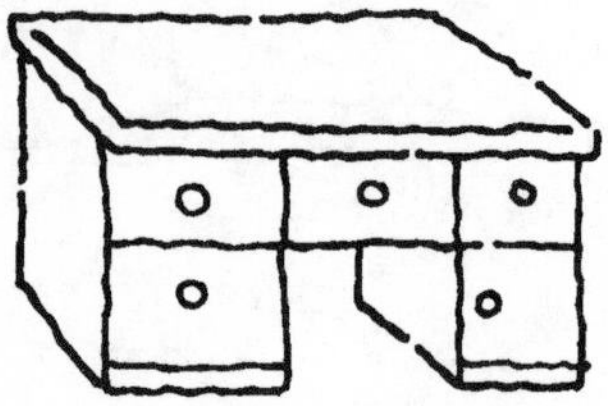
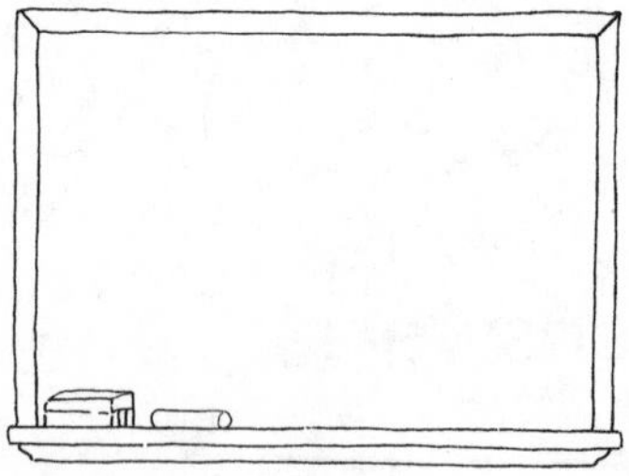

5.

ABC

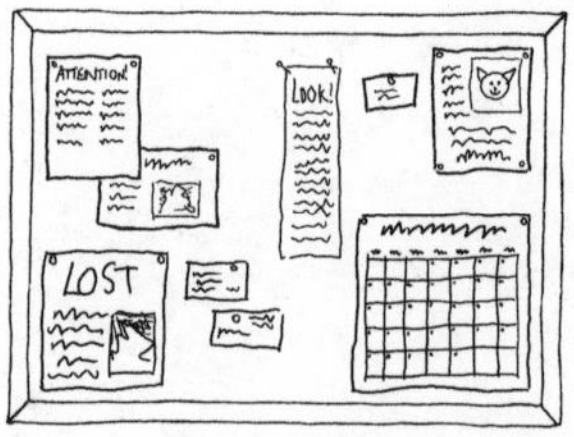
LOOK!
LOST

Score _____
(Top Score 5)

Teacher Have students look carefully at each group of pictures. Tell them to draw an X over the picture that does NOT belong.

Vocabulary List
1. desk
2. crayon
3. pencil
4. book
5. chalkboard
6. bulletin board
7. ruler
8. window
9. learn
10. listen

2 Reference Skills

Classroom Labeling

1.

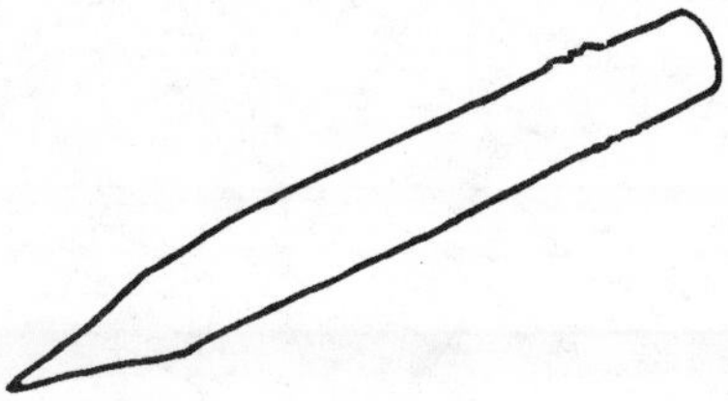

BOOK

2.

CRAYON

3.

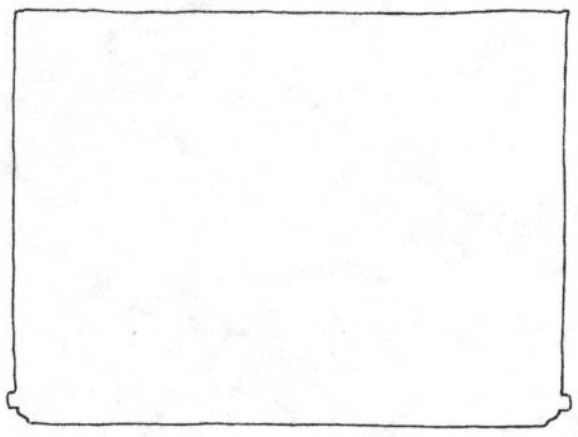

1 2 3 4 5 6 7 8 9 10 11
RULER

4.

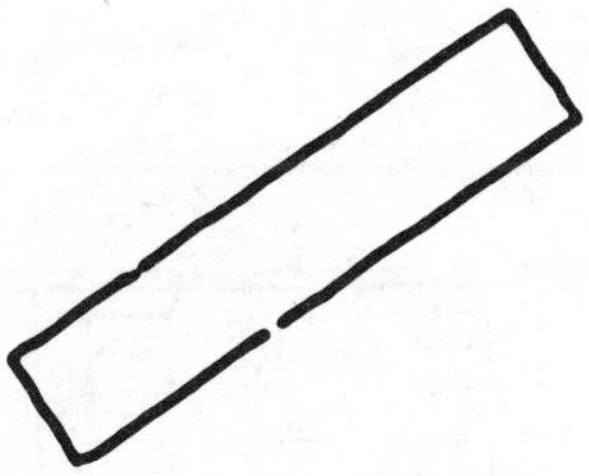

PENCIL

5.

CHALKBOARD

Teacher Have students look at each picture carefully. Tell them to draw a line from the outline of the picture on the left to the picture with the word label on it on the right.

Score ______
(Top Score 5)

3 Build New Vocabulary

Adding -s

1. pencils

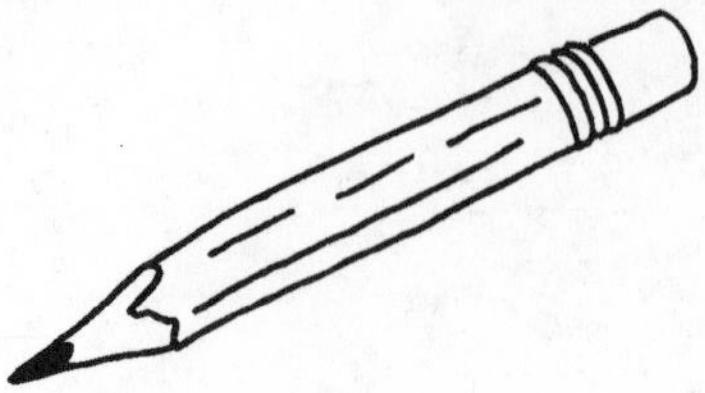

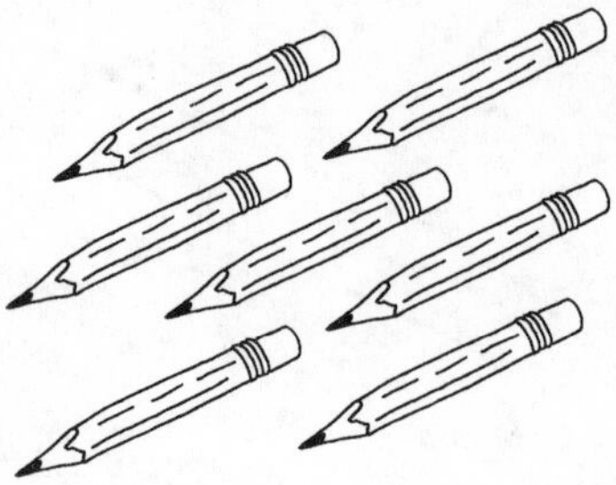

2. crayons

3. rulers

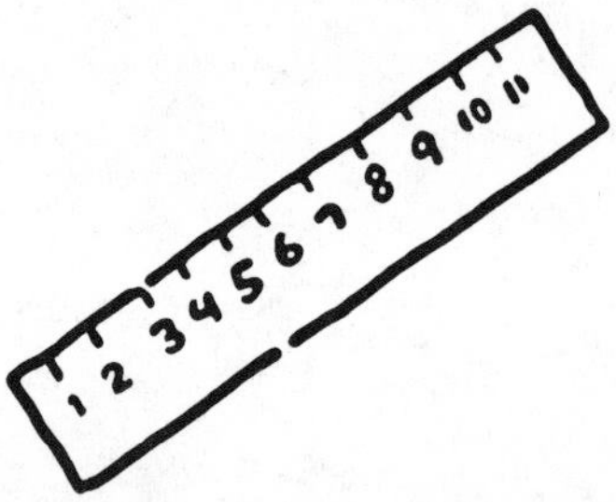

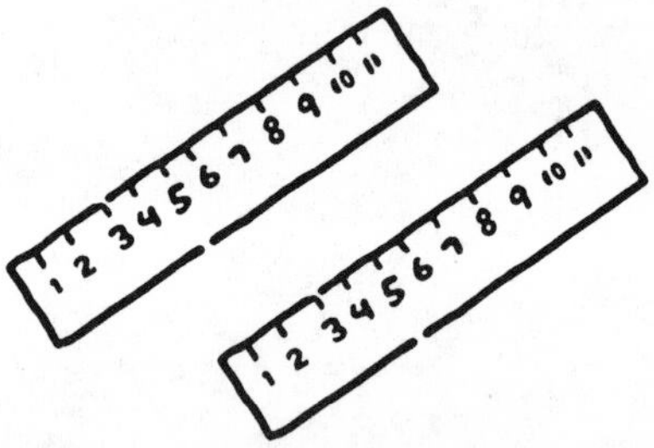

4. windows

5. books

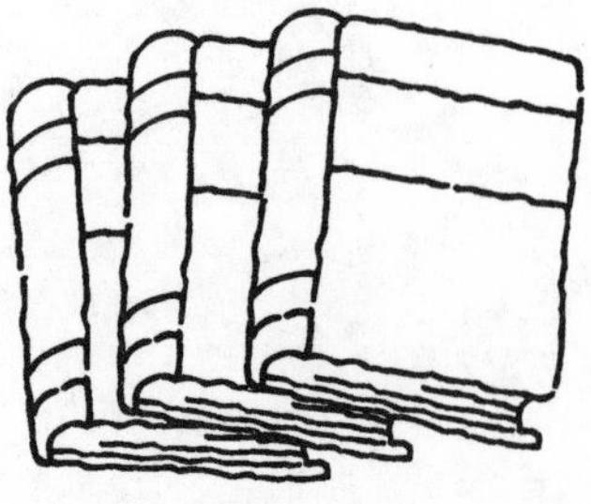

Three
Little
Pigs

Score ______
(Top Score 5)

Teacher Read each word aloud. Tell students to draw a circle around the picture that best matches the word.

Vocabulary List
1. desk
2. crayon
3. pencil
4. book
5. chalkboard
6. bulletin board
7. ruler
8. window
9. learn
10. listen

4 Word Play

Color Words

1. blue

2. red

3. orange

4. yellow

5. green

Teacher Read each color word aloud. Tell students to color in each crayon with the appropriate color.

Score ______
(Top Score 5)

Playground Vocabulary

1 Word Meanings

Examples

1. ball

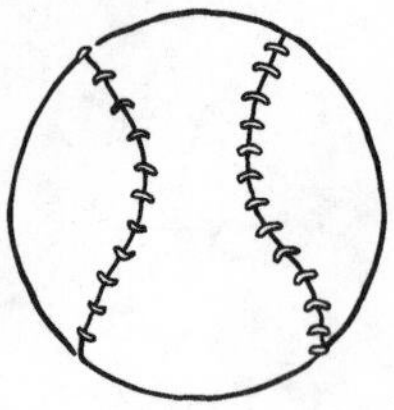
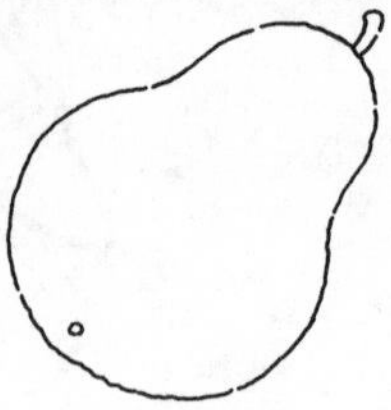

2. swing

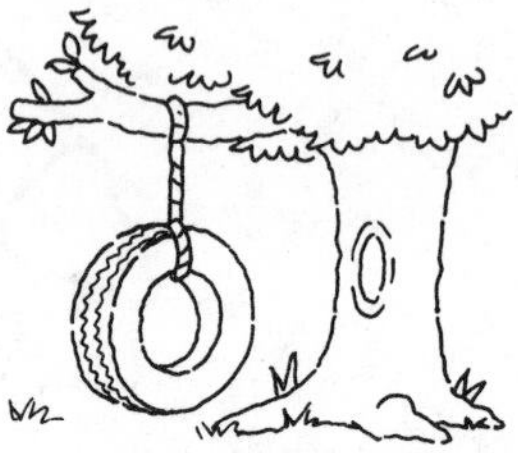
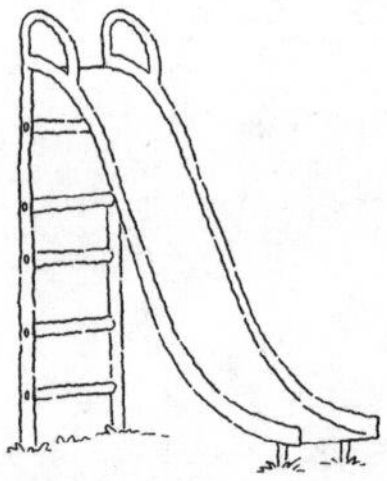

3. game

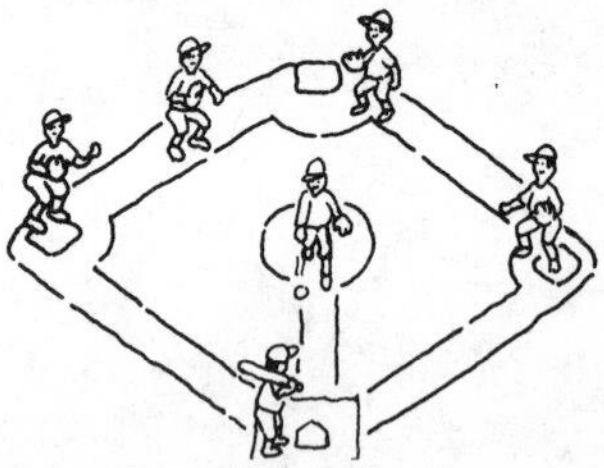

4. hop

5. climb

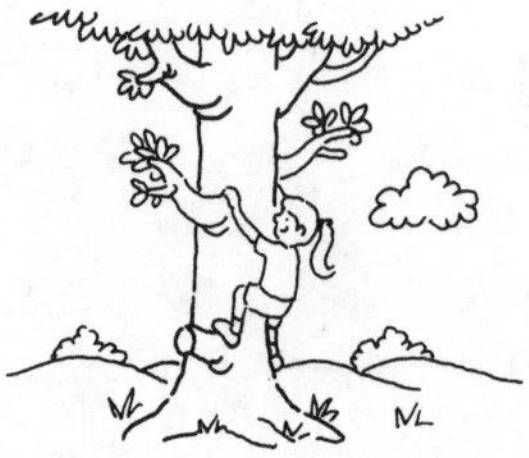

Score ______
(Top Score 5)

Teacher Read each word aloud. Tell students to draw an X over the picture that is NOT an example of the word.

Vocabulary List
1. ball
2. swing
3. climb
4. run
5. game
6. jump
7. hop
8. slide
9. bounce
10. hang

2 Reference Skills

Multiple Meanings

1. swing

2. slide

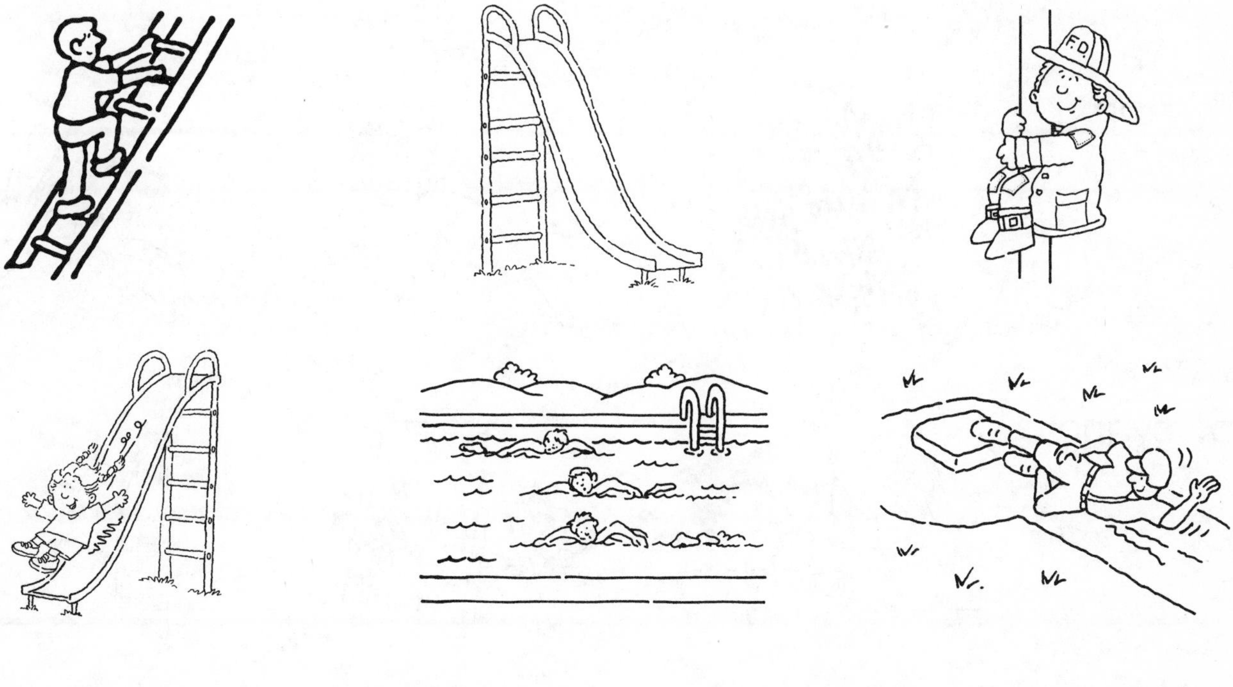

Teacher Read each word aloud. Tell students to draw an X over the pictures that do not match the word.

Score ______
(Top Score 4)

3 Build New Vocabulary

Action Words

1. run

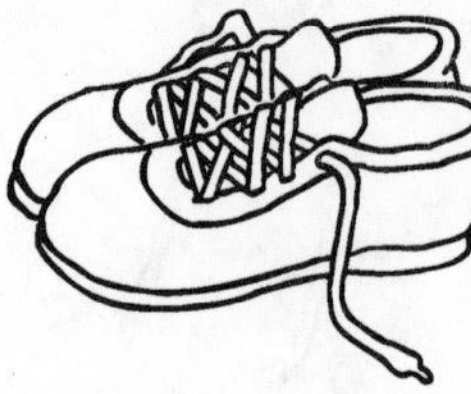

2. climb

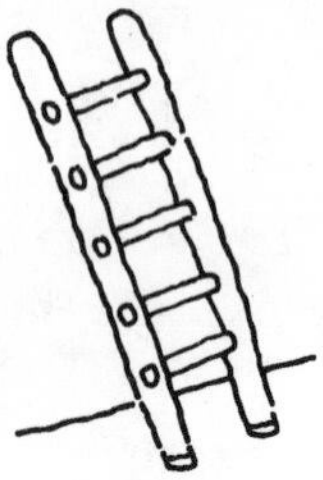
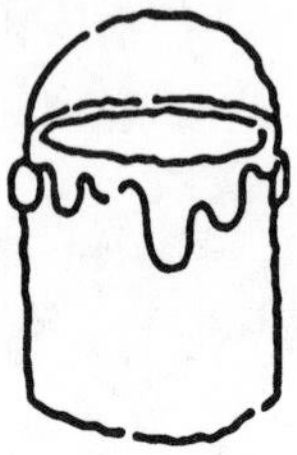

3. jump

4. hop

5. swing

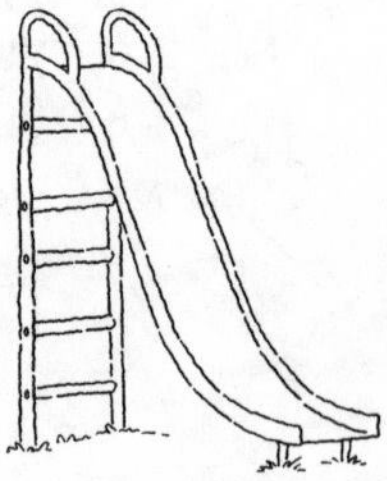

Score ______
(Top Score 5)

Teacher Read each action word aloud. Tell students to draw a circle around the picture that matches the word.

Vocabulary List
1. ball
2. swing
3. climb
4. run
5. game
6. jump
7. hop
8. slide
9. bounce
10. hang

4 Word Play

Rhyming Words

1. ball

2. run

3. jump

STOP

4. swing

5. hop

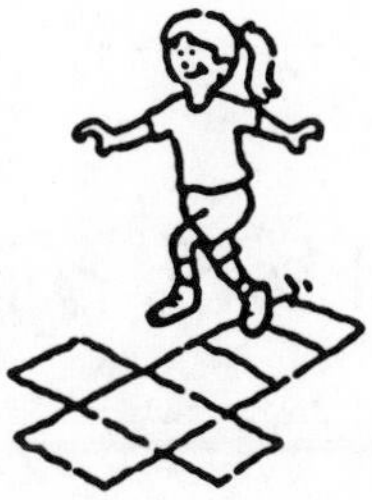

Teacher Read each word aloud. Tell students to draw a line from the picture in the left-hand column to the picture in the right-hand column that rhymes.

Score ______
(Top Score 5)

Question Words

1 Word Meanings

Using Question Words

1. Martin sat at the window watching the rain fall. *Who* sat at the window?

   Martin the rain

2. He wanted to go to the pool and swim. *Where* did he want to go?

   to swim to the pool

3. *What* did Martin want to do at the pool?

   swim watch the rain fall

4. His dad promised to take him to the pool that day, but then it started to rain. *When* was he supposed to go to the pool?

   that day because his dad had promised

5. *Why* wasn't Martin at the pool?

   he wanted to swim because it was raining

Score _____
(Top Score 5)

Teacher Read the following sentences, questions, and answer choices aloud. Tell students to listen carefully and circle the item that answers each question.

Vocabulary List
1. ask
2. what
3. how
4. when
5. where
6. who
7. why
8. which
9. because
10. if

2 Reference Skills

Word Wall

1. what	car
2. ask	apple
3. water	when
4. because	bed
5. inch	if
6. here	where
7. how	hop
8. cry	why

Teacher Read each pair of words aloud. Have students draw a line through the word that is NOT from the Vocabulary List.

Score ______
(Top Score 8)

3 Build New Vocabulary

Word Web

1. what

2. when

3. where

12
1
2
3
4
5
6
7
8
9
10
11

4. who

5. which

Three
Little
Pigs

Score ______
(Top Score 5)

Teacher Have students look carefully at each picture. Read each word aloud. Instruct students to draw a line from the word to the picture that best relates to the word.

Vocabulary List
1. ask
2. what
3. how
4. when
5. where
6. who
7. why
8. which
9. because
10. if

4 Word Play

Question Games

1. What has four legs?

2. Which book do you want?

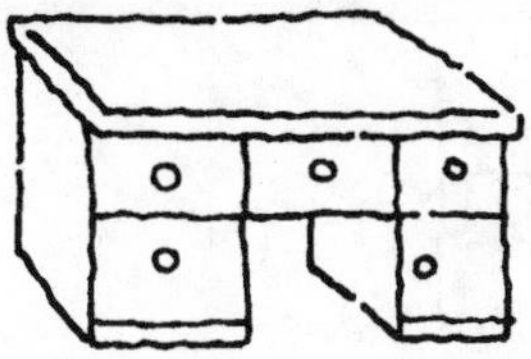

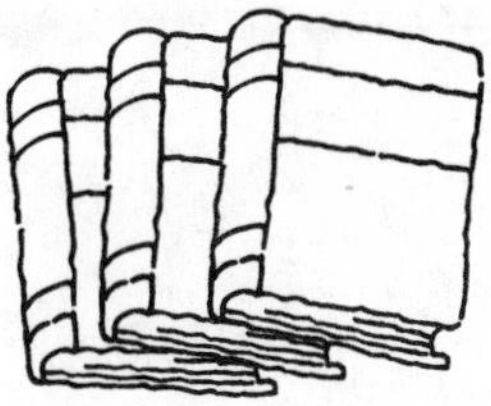

3. Where are you going?

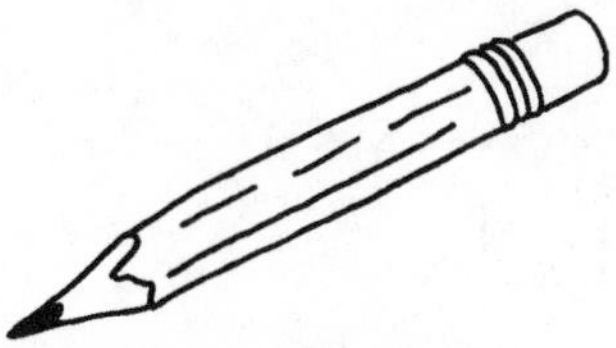

SCHOOL

4. When is lunchtime?

PEANUT
BUTTER

5. Who is your teacher?

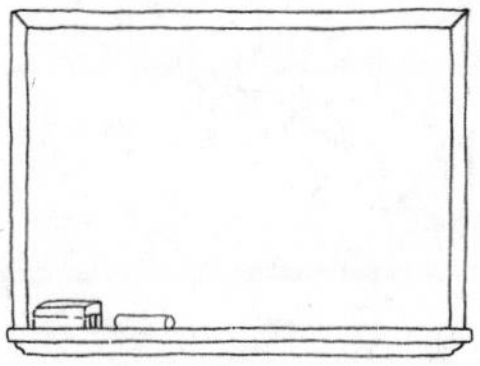

Teacher Read each question aloud. Instruct students to draw a circle around the picture that best relates to the question.

Score ______
(Top Score 5)

Vocabulary for Places

1 Word Meanings

Descriptions

1. park

$ BANK $

2. library

POST OFFICE
MAIL

3. market

BUS

4. firehouse

MUSEUM

STATION NO. 12

5. hospital

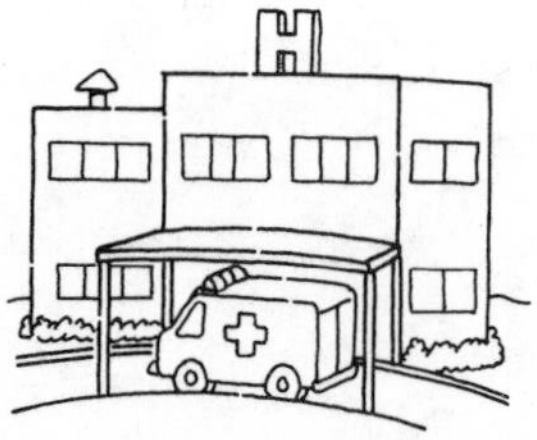

Score ______
(Top Score 5)

Teacher Read each word aloud. Tell students to draw a circle around the picture that matches the word.

Vocabulary List
1. park
2. bank
3. restaurant
4. library
5. bus stop
6. market
7. museum
8. firehouse
9. post office
10. hospital

2 Reference Skills

Picture Dictionary

1. bank

2. restaurant

POST OFFICE
MAIL

3. bus stop

$ BANK $

4. museum

MUSEUM

5. post office

BUS

Teacher Read each word aloud. Have students draw a line from the word on the left to the picture on the right that matches the word.

Score ______
(Top Score 5)

3 Build New Vocabulary

People and Places

1.

STATION NO. 12

ABC

2.

CITY BUS

3.

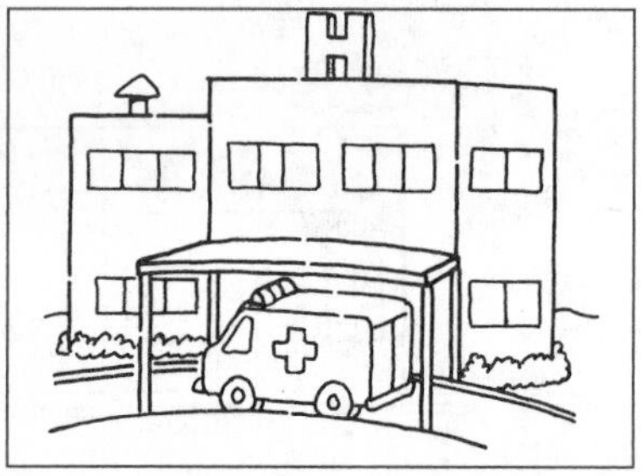
H

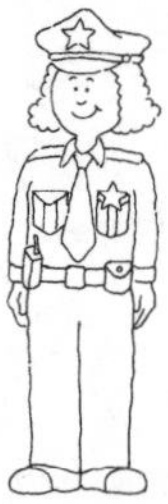

4.

POST OFFICE
MAIL

U.S. MAIL

5.

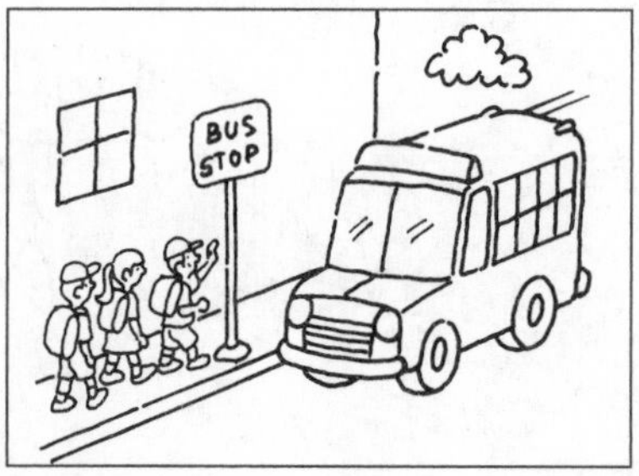
BUS STOP

CITY BUS

Score ______
(Top Score 5)

Teacher For each place picture, have students draw a circle around the picture of the person that belongs with that place.

Vocabulary List
1. park
2. bank
3. restaurant
4. library
5. bus stop
6. market
7. museum
8. firehouse
9. post office
10. hospital

4 Word Play

Silly Sentences

1. 

2. 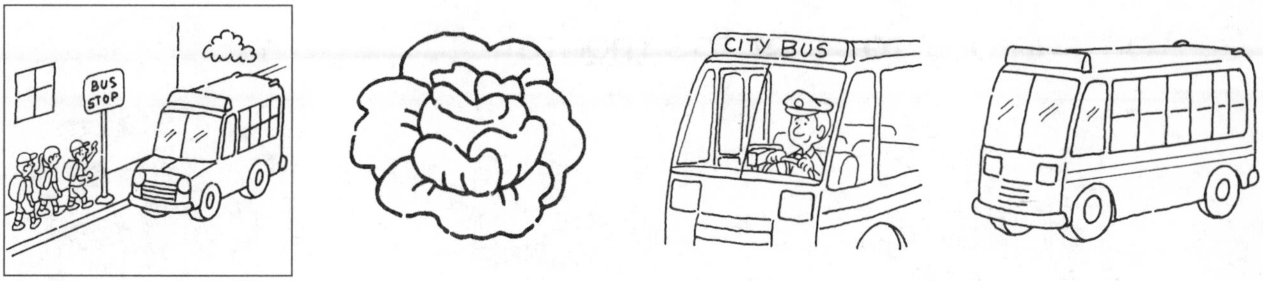
BUS STOP
CITY BUS

3. 

4. 
STATION NO. 12

5. 

Teacher For each place picture, have students draw an X over the picture that does NOT relate to the place.

Score ______
(Top Score 5)

Vocabulary Review

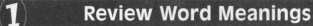

1 Review Word Meanings

1. I boarded the bus at the bus stop.

BUS

2. You can buy food at the market.

$ BANK $
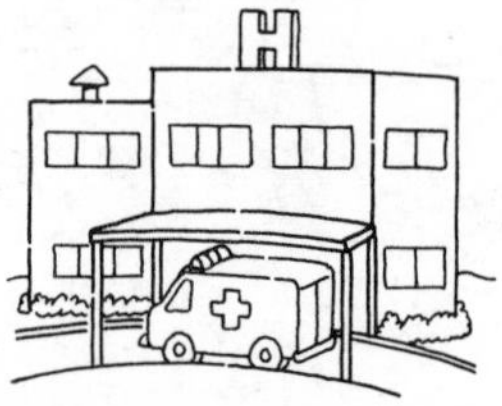
H

APPLES

3. Students learn in the classroom.

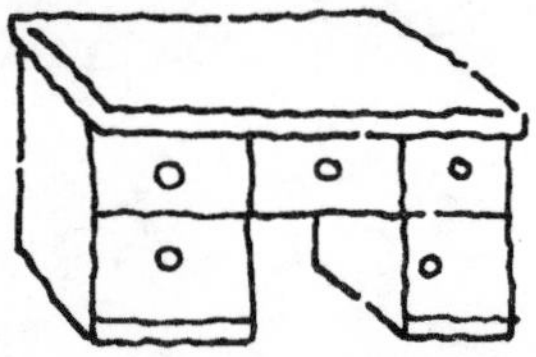

4. At school, I am a student.

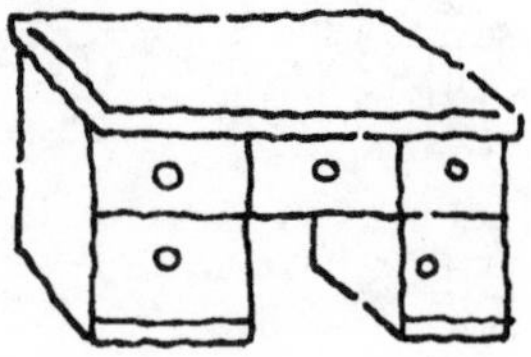
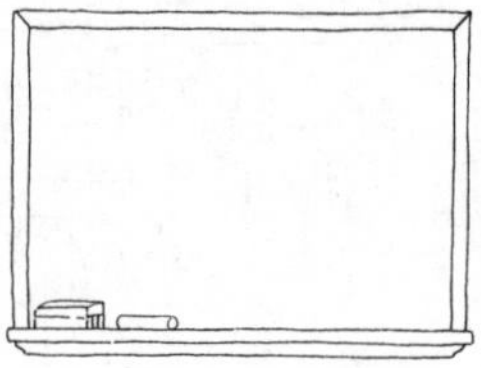

5. We are quiet during storytime.

HELLO
HI

Shhhh!

Score ______
(Top Score 5)

Teacher Read aloud the story on page 22 in the ***Teacher's Edition*** OR read the sentences above for each number. Tell students to draw a circle around the picture that best matches the underlined word.

2 Review Word Meanings

1. We write the alphabet.

2. We draw in our notebooks.

PEANUT BUTTER

3. Please read me that story.

Three Little Pigs

4. Think about the question.

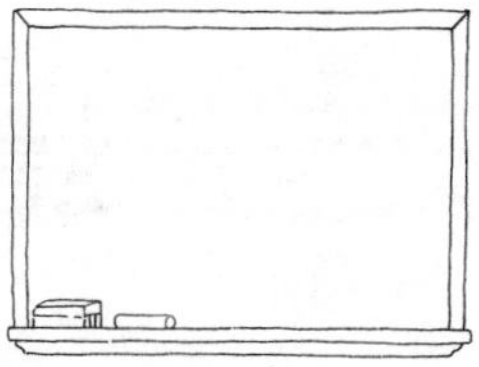

5. There are books at the library.

MUSEUM

STATION NO. 12

Teacher Read aloud the story on page 23 in the ***Teacher's Edition*** OR read the sentences above for each number. Tell students to draw a circle around the picture that best matches the underlined word.

Score ______
(Top Score 5)

3 Review Word Meanings

1. Who is that?

12
1
2
3
4
5
6
7
8
9
10
11

2. Alice can swing high and fast.

3. Let's play on the slide.

4. Can I borrow your pencil?

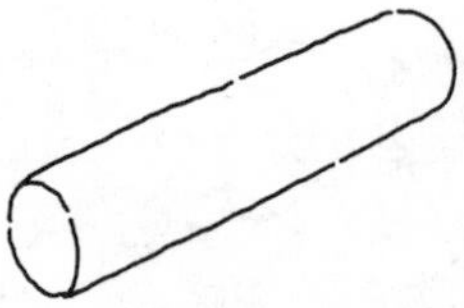
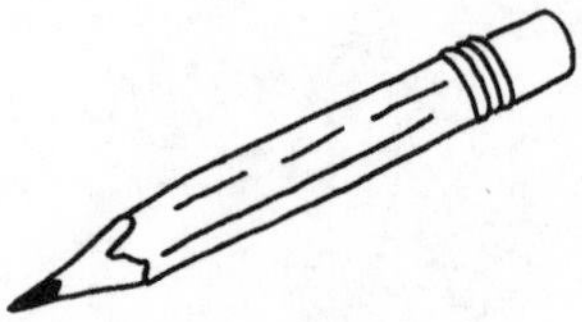

5. Use a ruler for measuring.

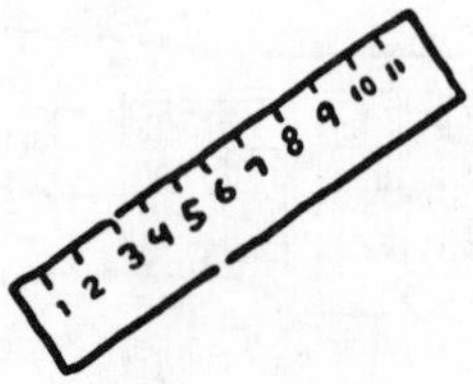
1 2 3 4 5 6 7 8 9 10 11
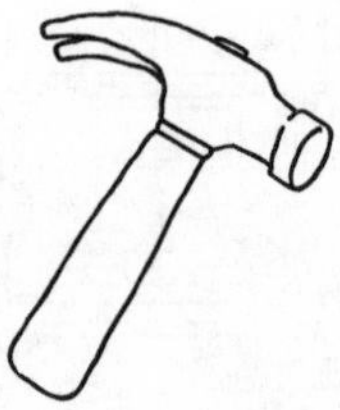

Score ______
(Top Score 5)

Teacher Read aloud the story on page 24 in the ***Teacher's Edition*** OR read the sentences above for each number. Tell students to draw a circle around the picture that best matches the underlined word.

4 Review Word Meanings

1. Look outside the window!

2. I lost my ball.

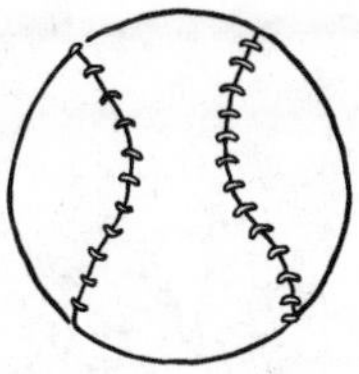

3. Can you run fast?

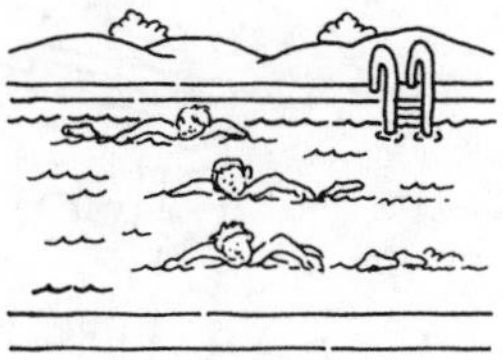

4. We jump in gym class.

5. My teacher is Mrs. Green.

ABC
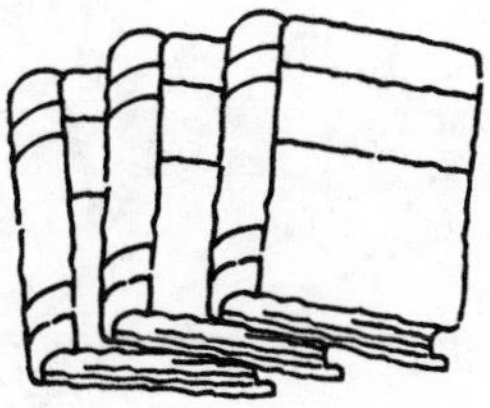

Teacher Read aloud the story on page 25 in the ***Teacher's Edition*** OR read the sentences above for each number. Tell students to draw a circle around the picture that best matches the underlined word.

Score ______
(Top Score 5)

"Shadows" Vocabulary

1 Word Meanings

Listening for Meaning

1. behind

2. follow

3. bright

BOOK

4. dark

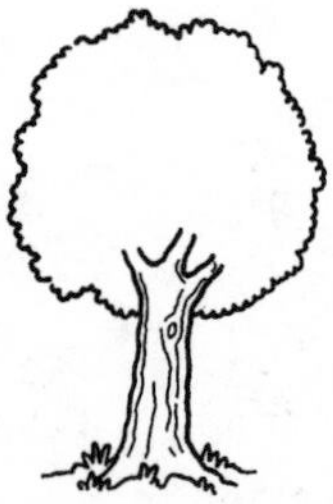

5. afraid

Score ______
(Top Score 5)

Teacher Read each word aloud. Tell students to draw a circle around the picture that best matches the word.

Vocabulary List
1. dark
2. bright
3. scare
4. follow
5. behind
6. appear
7. disappear
8. copy
9. own
10. afraid

2 Reference Skills

Synonyms

1. <u>afraid</u>

   glad   scared

2. <u>big</u>

   large   funny

3. <u>little</u>

   small   cuddle

4. <u>happy</u>

   mouth   glad

5. <u>jump</u>

   leap   run

Teacher Read each word and its answer choices aloud. Have students draw a circle around the word the means the same as the underlined word.

Score ______
(Top Score 5)

3 Build New Vocabulary

Opposites

1. wet

2. dark

3. tall

4. hot

5. up

A.

B.

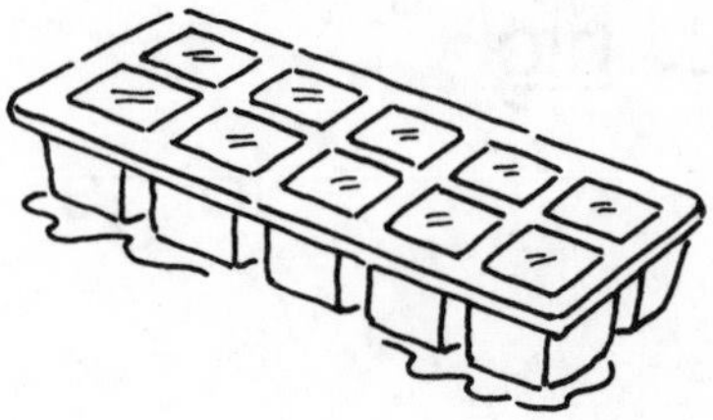

C.

D.

E.

Score ______
(Top Score 5)

Teacher Read each word aloud. Have students draw a line from the picture on the left to the picture on the right that best represents its opposite.

Vocabulary List

1. dark
2. bright
3. scare
4. follow
5. behind
6. appear
7. disappear
8. copy
9. own
10. afraid

4 Word Play

Tongue Twisters

1. copy

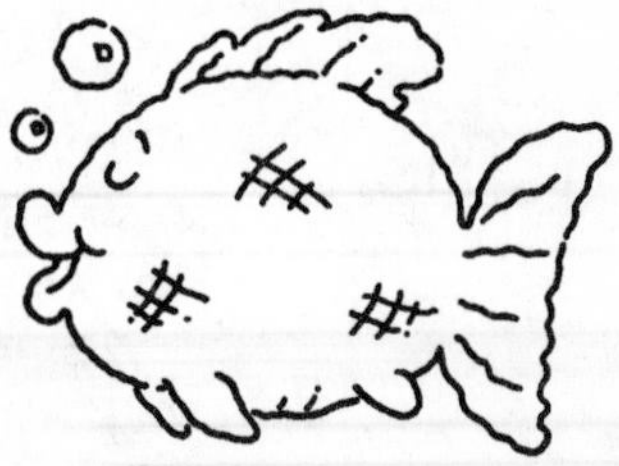

2. follow

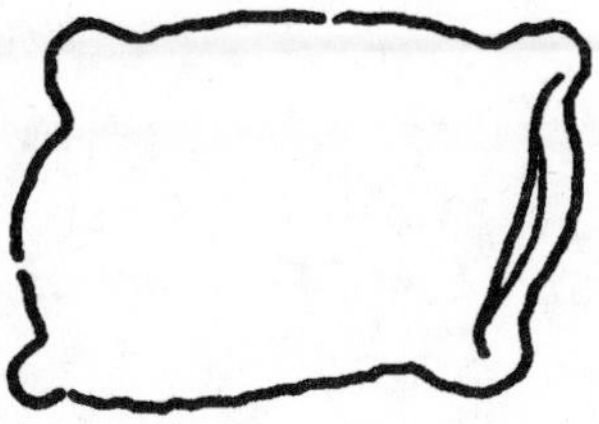

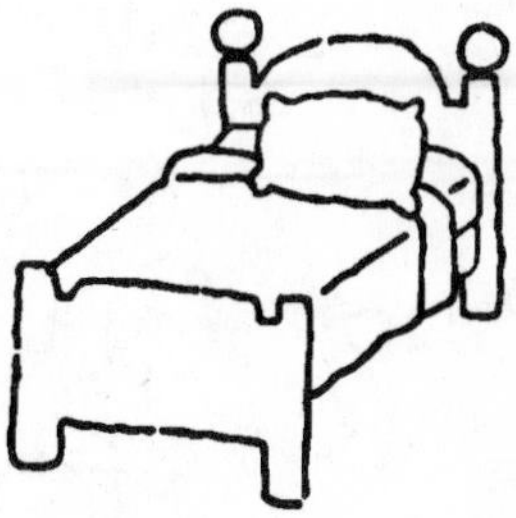

3. behind

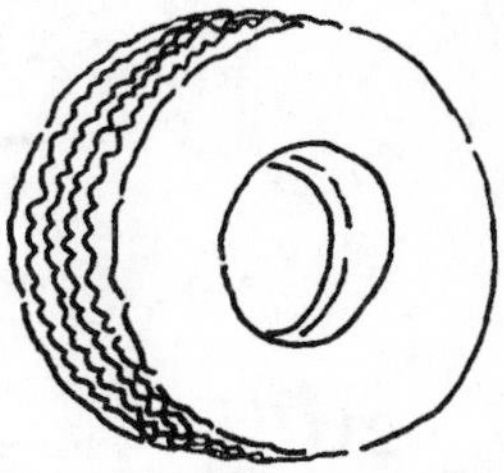

4. dark

5. scared

Teacher Read each word aloud. Have students draw a circle around the picture that begins with the same sound.

Score ______
(Top Score 5)

"Directions" Vocabulary

1 Word Meanings

Opposites Attract

1. up

2. to

3. off

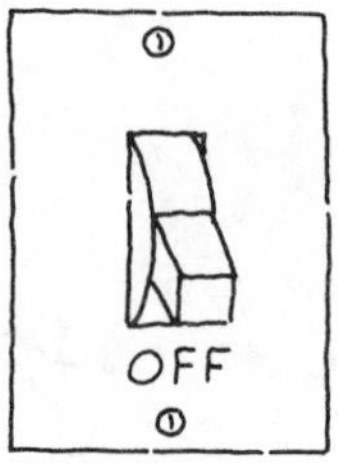
OFF

4. under

A. away

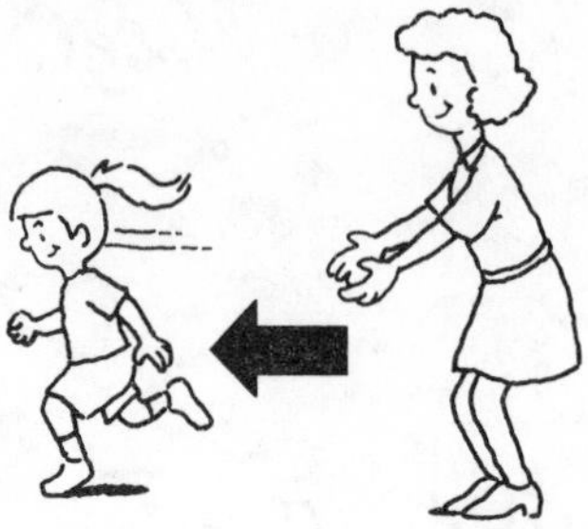

B. over

C. down

D. on

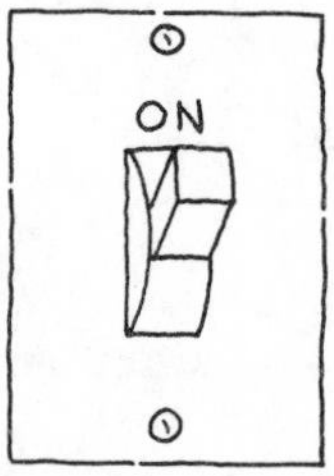
ON

Score ______
(Top Score 4)

Teacher Read each word aloud. Have students draw a line from the picture on the left to the picture on the right that best represents its opposite.

Vocabulary List
1. to
2. down
3. up
4. off
5. on
6. into
7. out
8. over
9. under
10. away

2 Reference Skills

Word Wall

1.

up under

2.

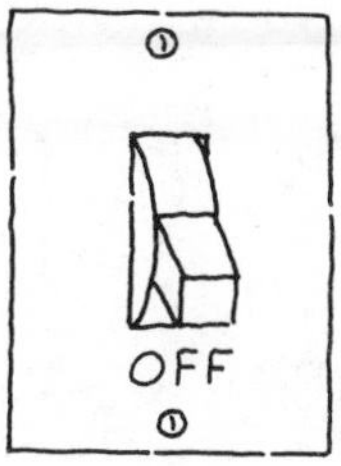
OFF

over off

3.

out to

4.

over down

5.

off under

Teacher Tell students to look at each picture closely. Read each answer choice aloud. Have students draw a circle around the word that best describes the picture.

Score ______
(Top Score 5)

3 Build New Vocabulary

Giving Directions

1. He ran down the ________________.

2. She went up the ________________.

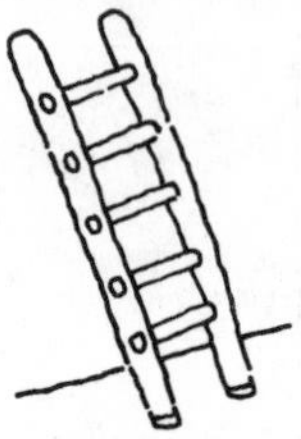

3. Please go to the ________________.

4. The car drove over the ________________.

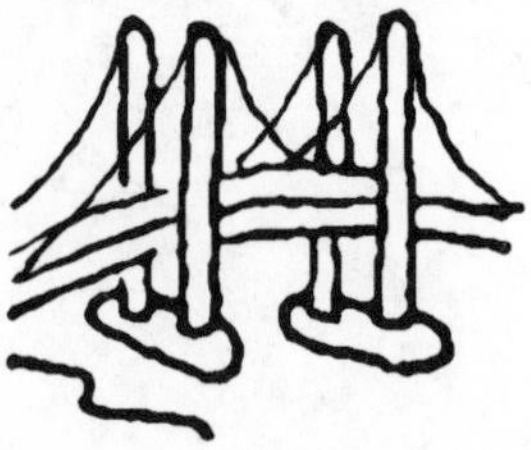

5. Put the money into the ________________.

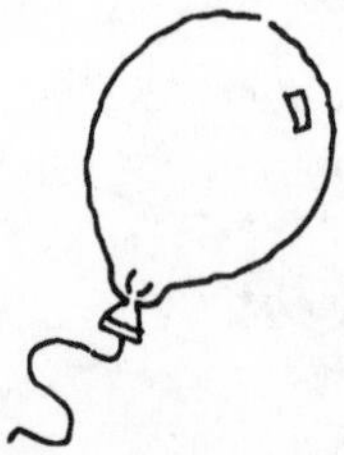

Score ______
(Top Score 5)

Teacher Read each incomplete sentence aloud. Have students draw a circle around the picture that best completes the sentence.

Vocabulary List
1. to
2. down
3. up
4. off
5. on
6. into
7. out
8. over
9. under
10. away

4 Word Play

Silly Rhymes

1.  

2.  

3.  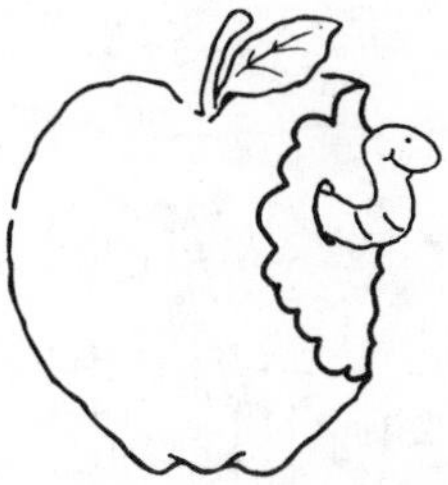

4.  

5.  

Teacher Tell students to look closely at each pair of pictures. Have them draw a circle around the picture that does NOT make sense.

Score _____
(Top Score 5)

Vocabulary for Seasons

1 Word Meanings

Categorization

1.

2.

3.

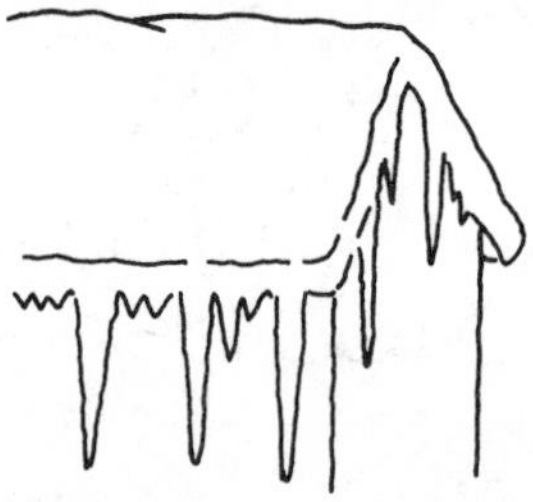

4.

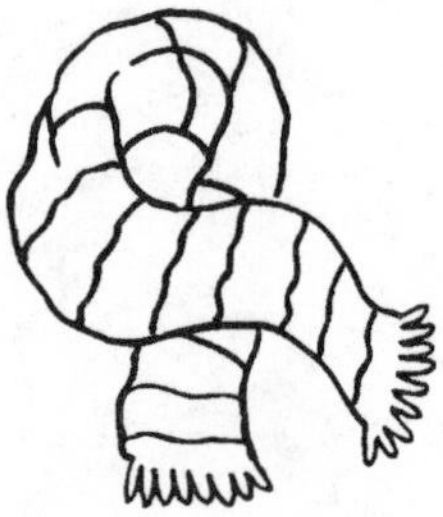

5.

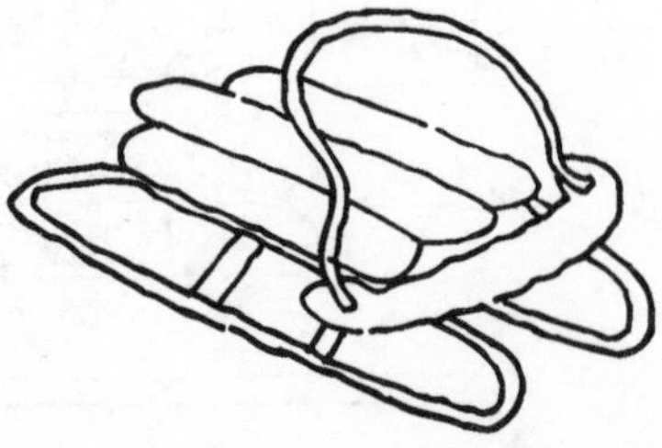

Score ______
(Top Score 5)

Teacher Tell students to look closely at each group of pictures. Have them draw an X over the picture that does NOT belong.

Vocabulary List
1. fall
2. autumn
3. corn
4. spring
5. bloom
6. summer
7. lazy
8. winter
9. snow
10. sled

2 Reference Skills

A Season Circle

1.  spring winter

2.  fall summer

3.  spring winter

4.  fall spring

5. 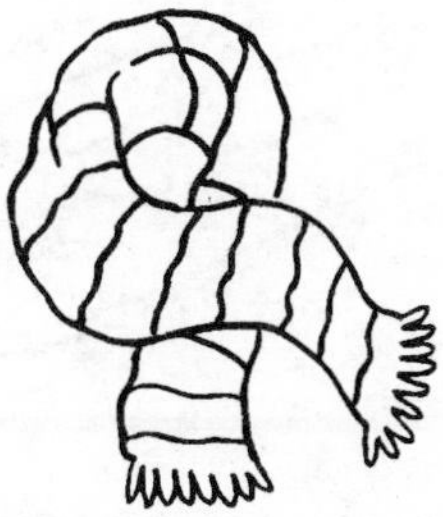 spring winter

Teacher Tell students to look at each picture closely. Read the answer choices aloud. Have students draw a circle around the word that best relates to the picture.

Score ______
(Top Score 5)

3 Build New Vocabulary

Words of the Season

WINTER

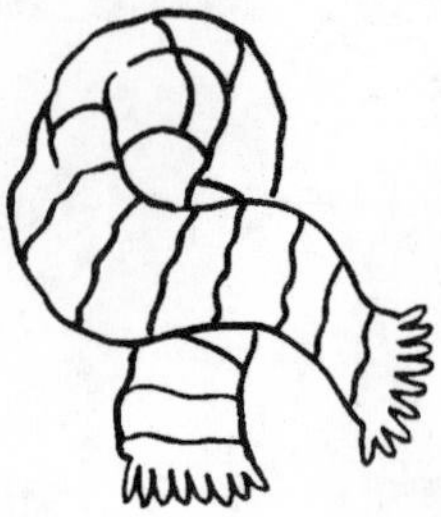

SPRING

SUMMER

FALL

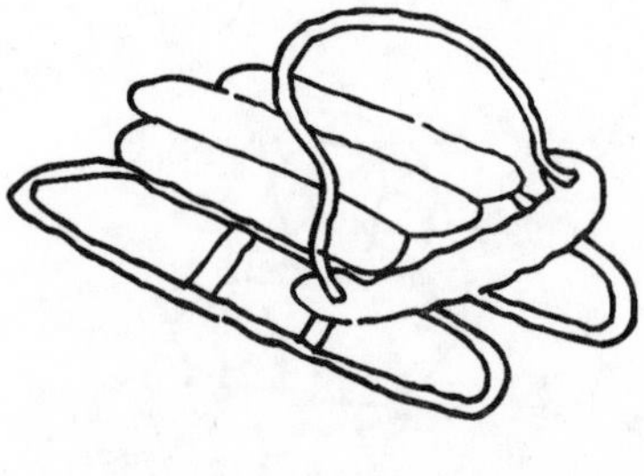

Score ______
(Top Score 4)

Teacher Have students look at each pair of pictures for each season. Have students circle the picture that best matches the season.

Vocabulary List

1. fall
2. autumn
3. corn
4. spring
5. bloom
6. summer
7. lazy
8. winter
9. snow
10. sled

4 Word Play

Word Families

1. wall	ball	call	will
2. wind	sing	ring	spring
3. row	snow	top	glow
4. side	by	ride	tide
5. take	lake	bake	love

Teacher Read each group of words aloud. Have students draw an X over the word that does NOT belong in the word family.

Score ______
(Top Score 5)

"Time Words" Vocabulary

1 Word Meanings

Using What I Know

1. stop

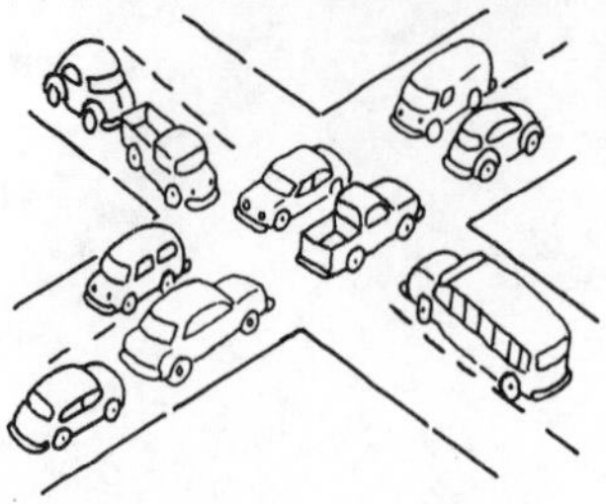

2. start

3. between

4. before

5. after

Score ______
(Top Score 5)

Teacher Tell students to look closely at each picture. Read each word aloud. Have students draw a circle around the picture that matches the word.

Vocabulary List		
1. after	3. never	7. start
2. before	4. between	8. stop
	5. once	9. now
	6. soon	10. again

2 Reference Skills

Alphabetical Order

1. after

2. between

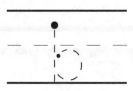

3. once

4. start

5. now

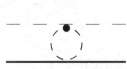

Teacher Read each word aloud. Tell students to draw a circle around the first letter of each word. Have students trace the letter provided on the lines. Then have students write the letters in alphabetical order.

Score ______
(Top Score 15)

3 Build New Vocabulary

How Often Does It Happen?

1. I could never do this!

2. This happens to me only once a year.

SCHOOL BUS

3. Which will happen to you soon?

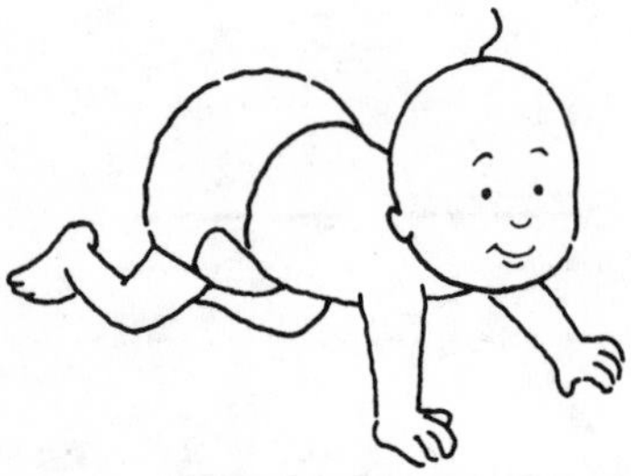

4. Which would you like to do again?

Score _____
(Top Score 4)

Teacher Tell students to look closely at each picture. Read each sentence aloud. Have students draw a circle around the picture that best relates to the underlined vocabulary word.

Vocabulary List
1. after
2. before
3. never
4. between
5. once
6. soon
7. start
8. stop
9. now
10. again

4 Word Play

Before and After

1.

2.

3.

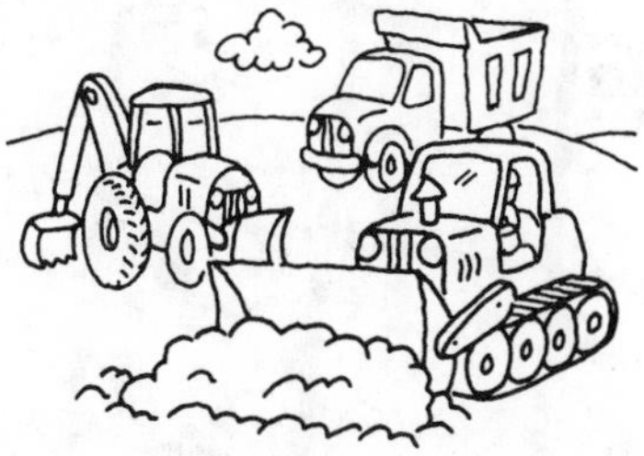

4.

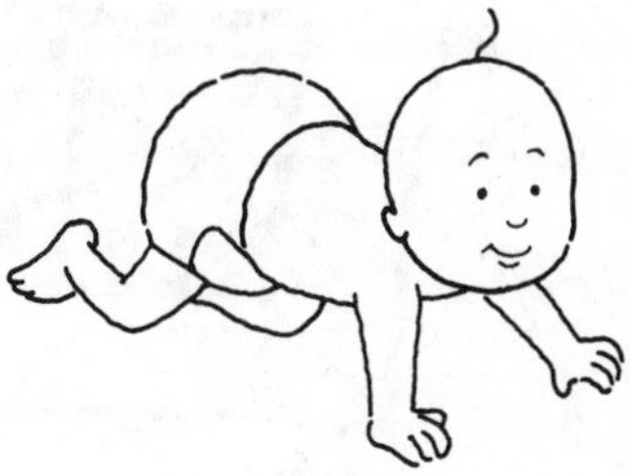

5.

Teacher Tell students to look closely at each picture. Have students draw a circle around the picture that happened BEFORE the other picture.

Score _____
(Top Score 5)

Calendar Vocabulary

1 Word Meanings

Learning Calendar Words

1. yesterday 2. tomorrow 3. week 4. weekend 5. month

JANUARY
S M T W T F S
1
2 3 4 5 6 7 8
9 10 11 12 13 14 15
16 17 18 19 20 21 22
23 24 25 26 27 28 29
30 31

Teacher Make sure each student has a blue, red, yellow, green, and purple crayon. Before beginning, select one day on the calendar to represent *today.* Have students mark an X on the appropriate calendar square. Read each numbered word aloud and tell students to color in the appropriate calendar squares. Color *yesterday* blue, *tomorrow* red, a *week* yellow, a *weekend* green, and trace the outline of the *month* in purple.

Score _____
(Top Score 5)

Vocabulary List		
1. today	3. tomorrow	7. year
2. yesterday	4. week	8. date
	5. weekend	9. plan
	6. month	10. mark

2 Reference Skills

Marking a Calendar

MAY
S M T W T F S
1
2
3
4
5
6
7
8
9
10
11
12
13
14
15
16
17
18
19
20
21
22
23
24
25
26
27
28
29
30
31

Teacher Make sure each student has a green, yellow, red, pink, and purple crayon. Have them color the appropriate day(s) as you read the following aloud: 1) *Color the first day of the month green;* 2) *Color the* weekend *that the soccer game is planned yellow;* 3) *Color the day a fire drill is planned red;* 4) *Color Mother's Day (represented by flowers) pink;* 5) *Color the* week *that the dentist appointment is scheduled purple.*

Score ______
(Top Score 5)

3 Build New Vocabulary

Root Words

day

1. birthday

2. today

3. yesterday

4. daylight

5. daytime

6. holiday

7. Monday

8. Friday

JANUARY
S M T W T F S
1 2 3 4 5 6 7 8 9 10 11 12 13 14 15 16 17 18 19 20 21 22 23 24 25 26 27 28 29 30 31

Score ______
(Top Score 8)

Teacher Read each word aloud. Have students draw a circle around the root word *day* in each word.

Vocabulary List
1. today
2. yesterday
3. tomorrow
4. week
5. weekend
6. month
7. year
8. date
9. plan
10. mark

4 Word Play

Happy Birthday!

1. August is a ____________________.

today   month

2. Seven days make up a ____________________.

week   tomorrow

3. Twelve months make up a ____________________.

weekend   year

4. The teacher will ____________________ everyone's birthday on the class calendar.

mark   yesterday

5. Saturday and Sunday are called a ____________________.

date   weekend

Teacher Read each incomplete sentence aloud. Have students draw a circle around the word that best completes the sentence.

Score ______
(Top Score 5)

Vocabulary Review

1 Review Word Meanings

1. The weather is cold during the winter.

2. The weather is warm during the spring.

3. Leaves change color during the fall.

4. Today is a bright, sunny day.

5. The sun stayed behind the clouds all day.

Score ______
(Top Score 5)

Teacher Read aloud the story on page 46 in the ***Teacher's Edition*** OR read each sentence above for each number. Tell students to draw a circle around the picture that best matches the underlined word.

2 Review Word Meanings

1. There is a lot of <u>snow</u> covering the ground.

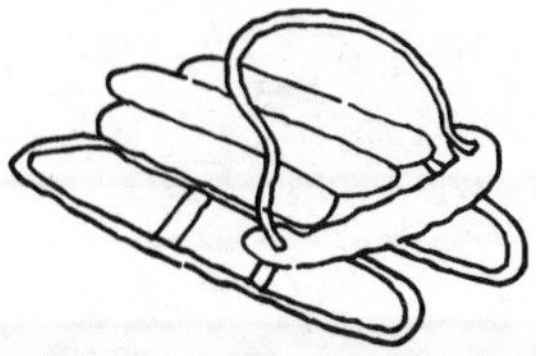
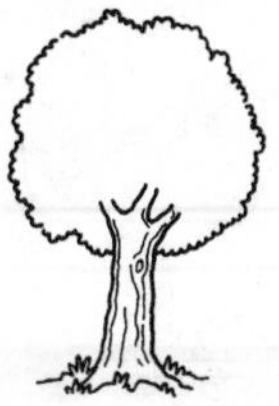

2. As I sled <u>down</u> the hill, my shadow follows me.

3. As I sled down the hill, my shadow <u>follows</u> me.

4. I am not allowed to sled when it is <u>dark</u> outside.

5. Tomorrow my cousins will visit and stay all <u>weekend</u>.

JANUARY

JANUARY

JANUARY

Teacher Read aloud the story on page 47 in the *Teacher's Edition* OR read each sentence above for each number. Tell students to draw a circle around the picture that best matches the underlined word.

Score ______
(Top Score 5)

3 Review Word Meanings

1. The new flowers in <u>bloom</u> make unique shadows.

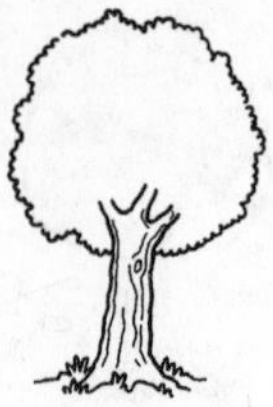
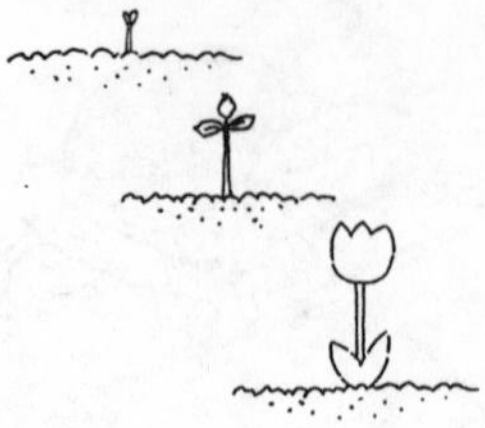

2. I raise my arms <u>over</u> the top of my head as if they were petals.

3. May is my favorite <u>month</u> of spring.

JANUARY
S M T W T F S

JANUARY
S M T W T F S

JANUARY
S M T W T F S

4. In the summer, my family spends a <u>week</u> at the beach.

JANUARY
S M T W T F S

JANUARY
S M T W T F S

JANUARY
S M T W T F S

5. The seagull flew <u>away</u> before I could see its shadow.

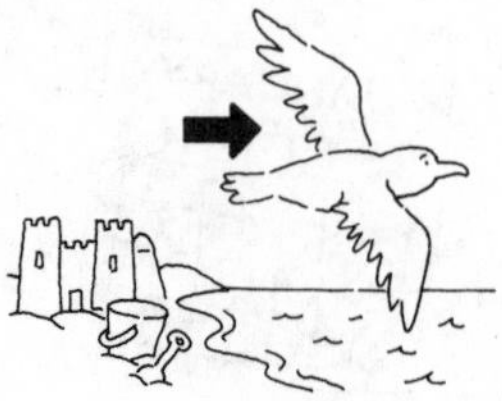

Score ______
(Top Score 5)

Teacher Read aloud the story on page 48 in the ***Teacher's Edition*** OR read each sentence above for each number. Tell students to draw a circle around the picture that best matches the underlined word.

4 Review Word Meanings

1. The trees make scary shadows, but I am not afraid.

2. We hide under the leaves and jump out.

3. Then my brother and I go to Farmer Murray's field of corn.

4. We play hide and seek between the stalks.

5. I use a calendar to mark the date I see a new shadow.

JANUARY

JANUARY

Teacher Read aloud the story on page 49 in the *Teacher's Edition* OR read each sentence above for each number. Tell students to draw a circle around the picture that best matches the underlined word.

Score ______
(Top Score 5)

"Finding Friends" Vocabulary

1 Word Meanings

Showing Meanings

1. share	A. 
2. laugh	B. SALE $
3. funny	C. 
4. play	D. 
5. new	E. 

Score _____
(Top Score 5)

Teacher Read each word aloud. Have students draw a line from each word to the picture that best matches.

Vocabulary List		
1. kind	3. like	7. funny
2. laugh	4. new	8. play
	5. old	9. care
	6. best	10. share

2 Reference Skills

Alphabetical Order

1. best

2. like

3. care

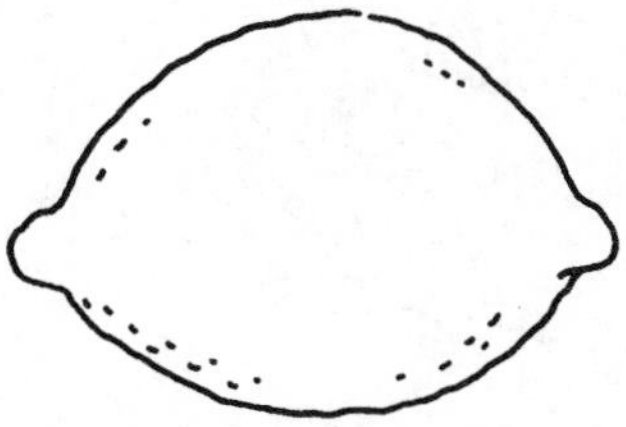

4. kind

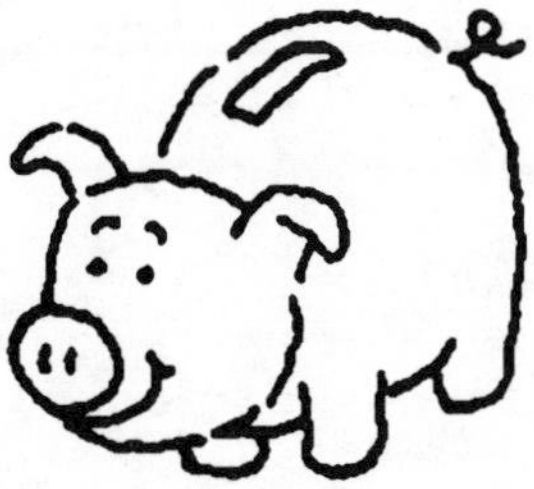
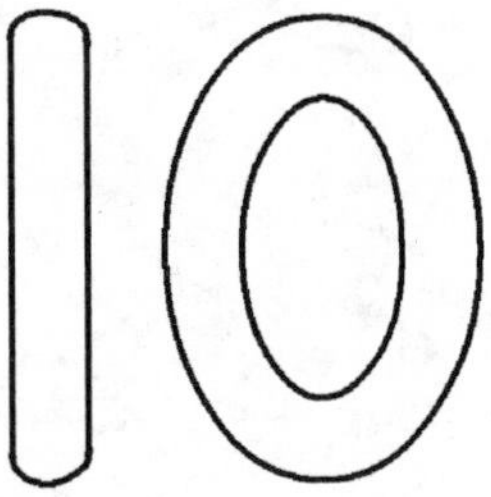

5. funny

Teacher Read each word aloud and point out the letters to students. Have them draw a circle around the picture that begins with the same letter as the word.

Score _____
(Top Score 5)

3 Build New Vocabulary

The Best of *-est*

1. kind

A. oldest

2. soft

B. fastest

3. old

C. kindest

4. fast

D. slowest

5. slow

E. softest

Score ______
(Top Score 5)

Teacher Read each word aloud. Have students look at each picture and have them draw a line from the picture to the *-est* form of the word.

Vocabulary List		
1. kind	3. like	7. funny
2. laugh	4. new	8. play
	5. old	9. care
	6. best	10. share

4 Word Play

Describing Best Friends

1. She sees the funny ______________.

2. He likes to eat ______________.

3. We love to play ______________.

4. Have you met the new ______________?

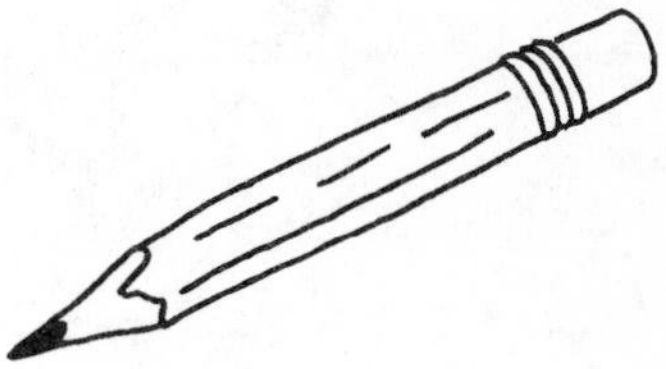

5. Please share your ______________.

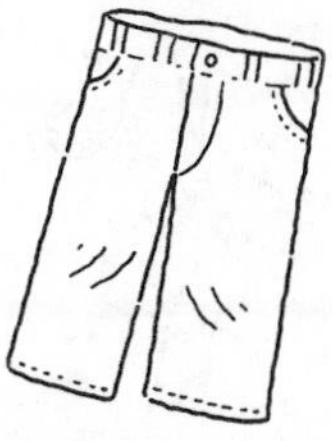

Teacher Read each incomplete sentence aloud. Have students draw a circle around the picture that best completes the sentence.

Score ______
(Top Score 5)

Vocabulary About Me

1 Word Meanings

Reading a Friendly Letter

1. address

A.

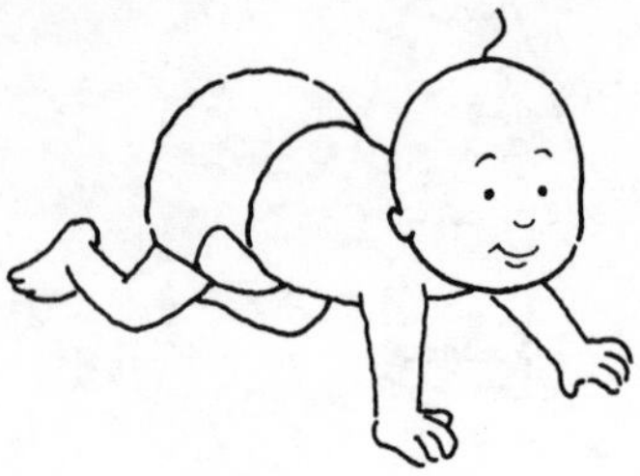

2. happy

B.

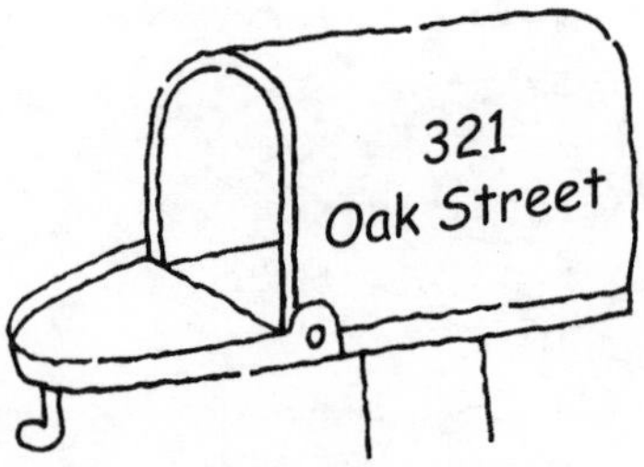
321
Oak Street

3. sad

C.

4. young

D.

5. age

E.

Score ______
(Top Score 5)

Teacher Read each word aloud. Have students draw a line from the word to the picture that best matches.

Vocabulary List		
1. address	3. age	7. want
2. from	4. young	8. well
	5. good	9. happy
	6. very	10. sad

2 Reference Skills

Thesaurus Rex

1. happy

2. sad

3. well

4. want

5. young

A. gloomy

B. choose

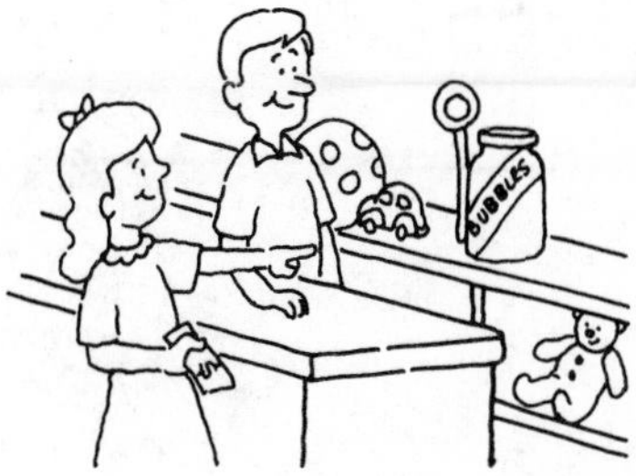

BUBBLES

C. glad

D. little

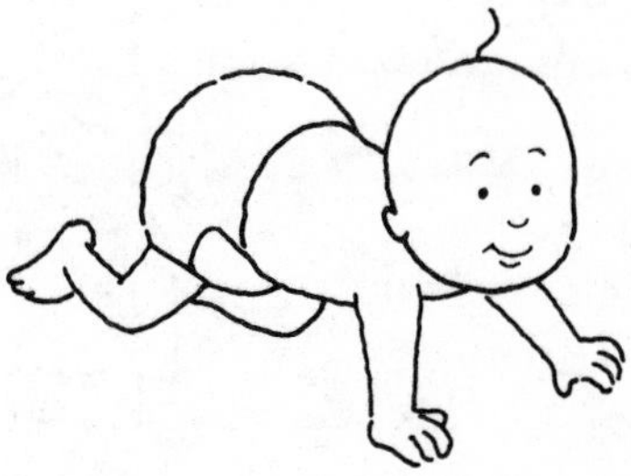

E. healthy

Teacher Read each word aloud. Have students draw a line from the word on the left to the synonym and picture that matches.

Score ______
(Top Score 5)

3 Build New Vocabulary

Feelings

1. mad

2. tired

3. happy

4. sad

5. scared

Score ______
(Top Score 5)

Teacher Read each word aloud. Have students draw a circle around the picture that best represents the feeling.

Vocabulary List

1. address
2. from
3. age
4. young
5. good
6. very
7. want
8. well
9. happy
10. sad

4 Word Play

Write a Friendly Letter

1. I am the age of ______________.

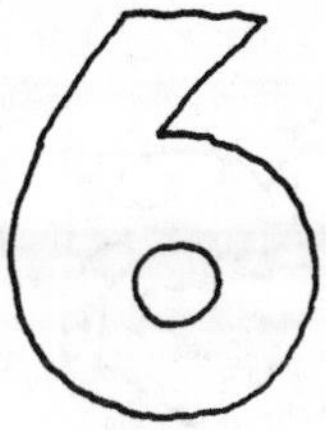
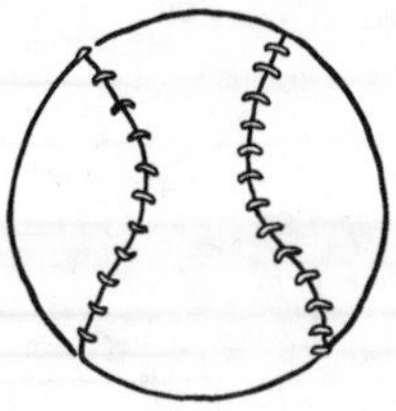

2. The address is on the ______________.

3. I want to eat ______________.

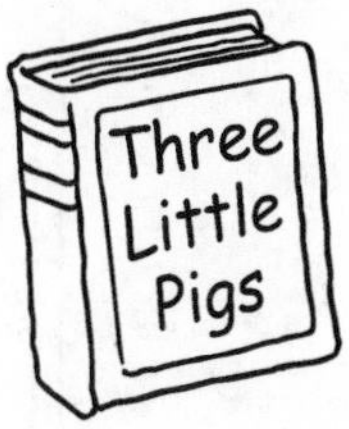
Three
Little
Pigs

4. The letter is from my ______________.

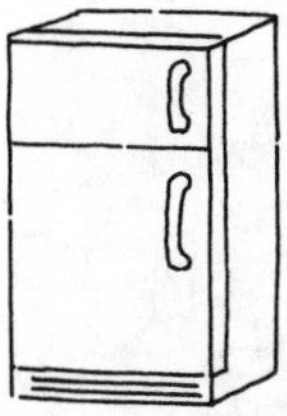

5. She plays the ______________ well.

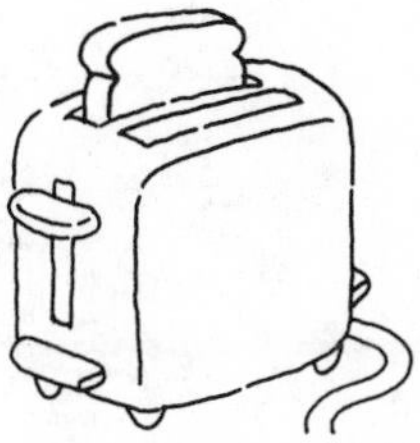

Teacher Read each sentence aloud. Have students draw a circle around the picture that best completes each sentence.

Score ______
(Top Score 5)

Vocabulary for Home

1 Word Meanings

Compare and Contrast

1. chair

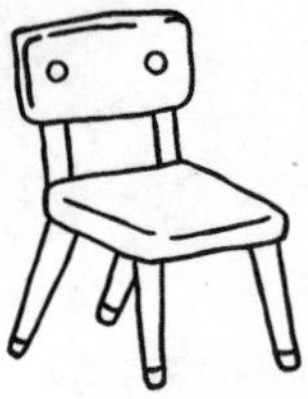

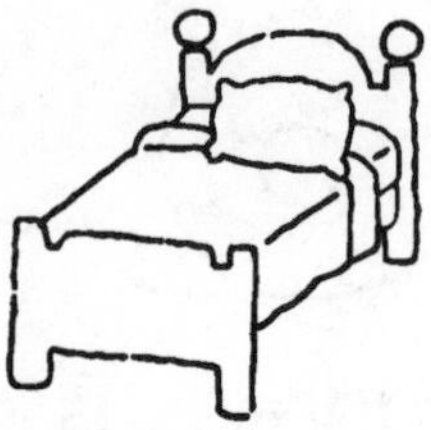

2. kitchen

3. bed

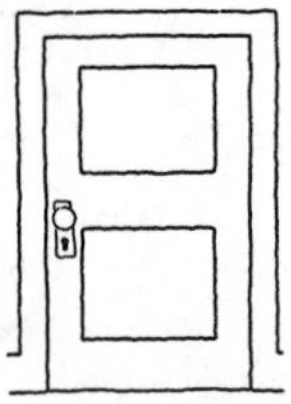

4. closet

5. fireplace

Score ____
(Top Score 5)

Teacher Read each word aloud. Have students compare each set of pictures and then draw a circle around the picture that matches the word.

Vocabulary List
1. chair
2. bed
3. backyard
4. bathroom
5. fireplace
6. room
7. closet
8. kitchen
9. door
10. floor

2 Reference Skills

Picture Dictionary

1. backyard

A. 

2. bathroom

B. 

3. door

C. 

4. bed

D. 

5. floor

E. 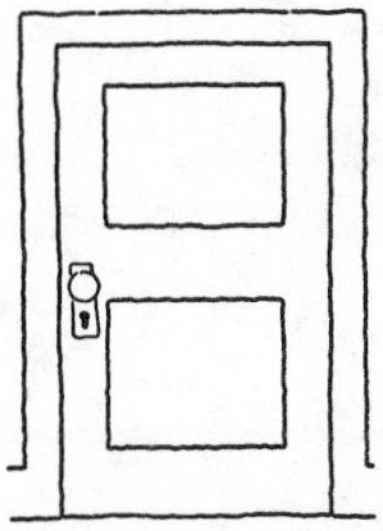

Teacher Read each word aloud. Have students draw a line from each vocabulary word to the picture that best matches.

Score ______
(Top Score 5)

3 Build New Vocabulary

Compound Words

1. chair

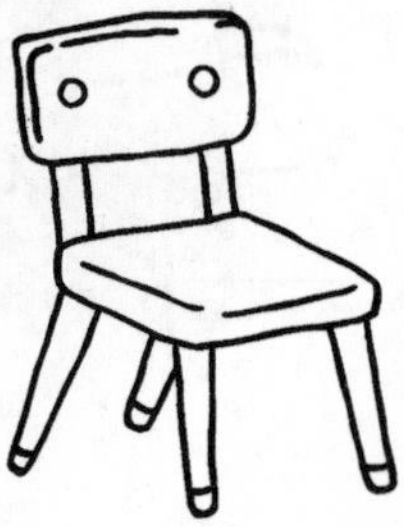

backyard

2. fireplace

bed

3. door

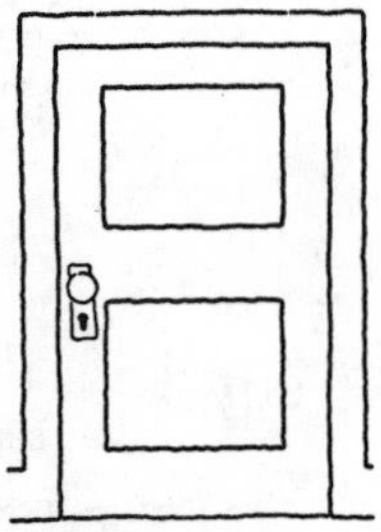

bathroom

4. bedroom

GO TEAM

kitchen

Score ______
(Top Score 4)

Teacher Have students look at each pair of words as you read them aloud. Tell students to circle the word that is a large, or compound, word that is made up of two smaller words.

Vocabulary List
1. chair
2. bed
3. backyard
4. bathroom
5. fireplace
6. room
7. closet
8. kitchen
9. door
10. floor

4 Word Play

What's in My Home?

1. backyard

 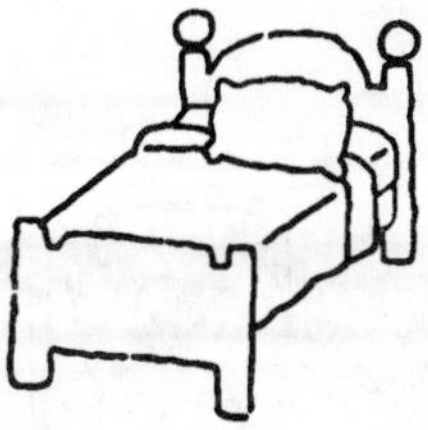 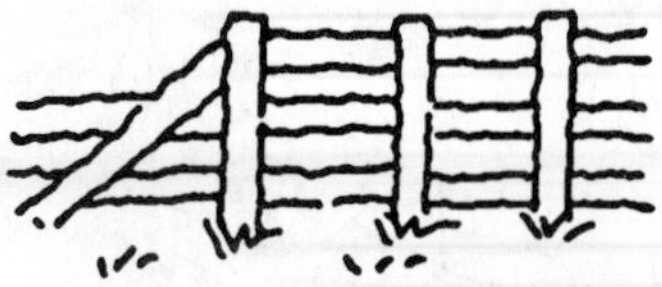

2. bathroom

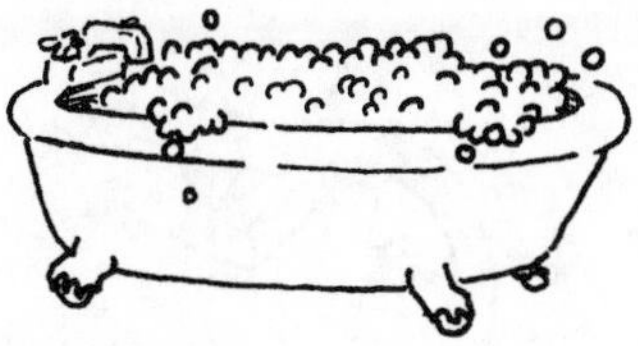 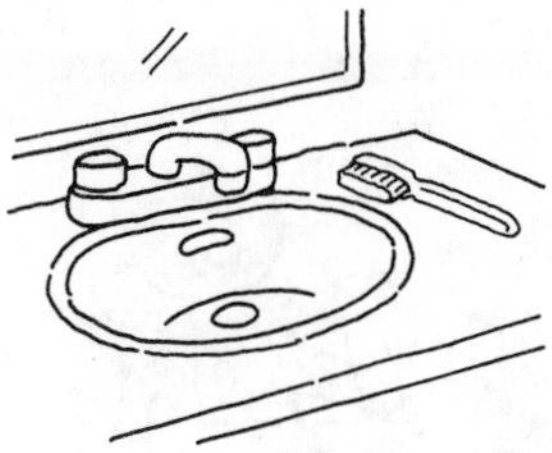 

3. kitchen

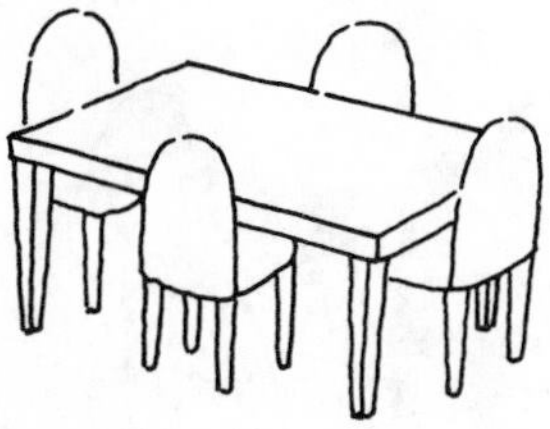 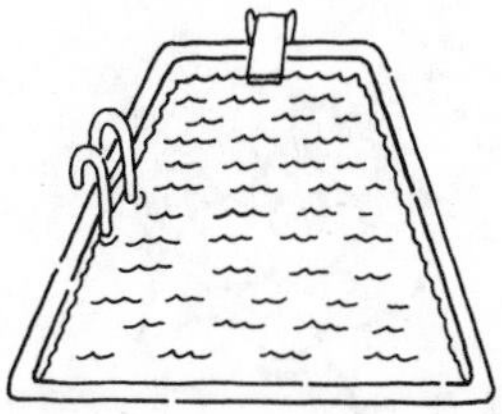 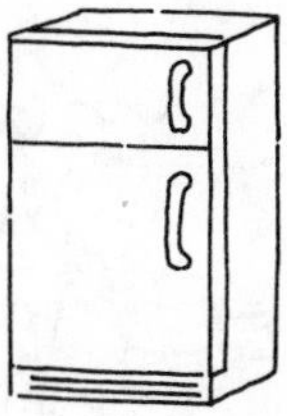

4. closet

 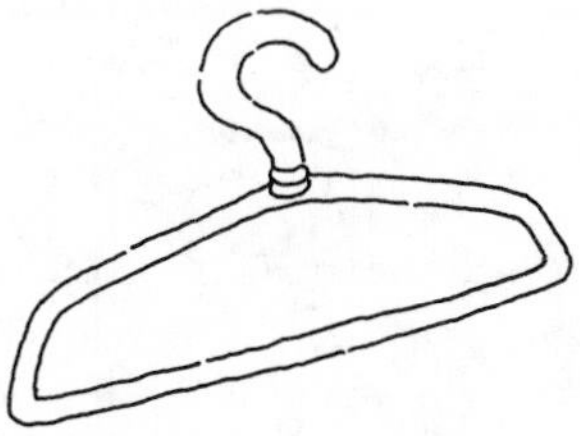 

5. bed

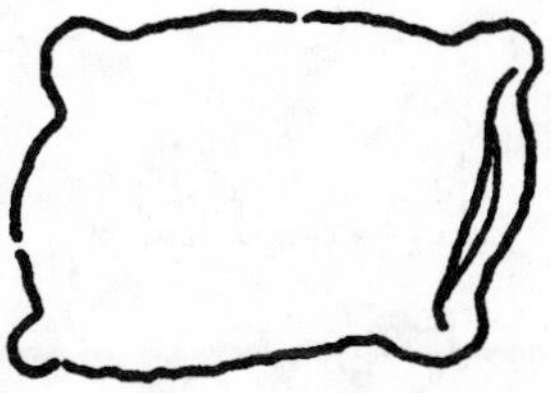  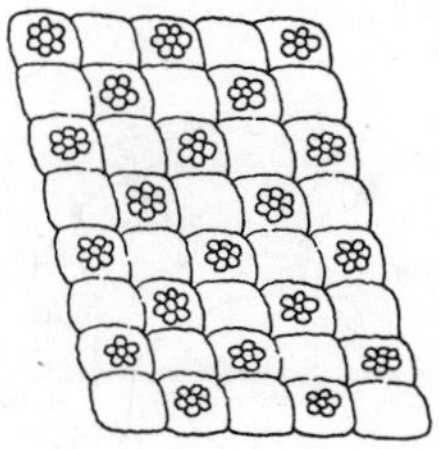

Teacher Read each word aloud. Have students draw a circle around the two pictures that relate to the word.

Score ______
(Top Score 5)

"My Day" Vocabulary

1 Word Meanings

What I Did Today

1. wake

2. eat

3. drink

4. wash

5. sleep

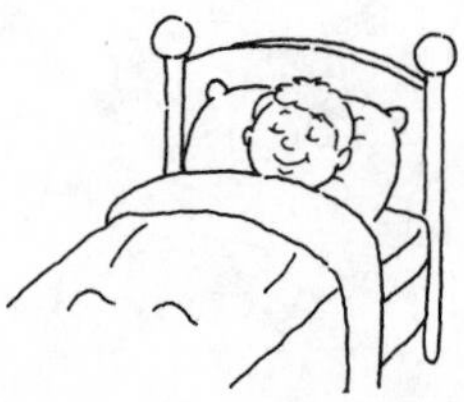  

Score ______
(Top Score 5)

Teacher Read each word aloud. Have students draw a circle around the picture that best matches the word.

Vocabulary List

1. wake
2. morning
3. eat
4. drink
5. lunch
6. afternoon
7. wash
8. dinner
9. sleep
10. night

2 Reference Skills

Which Is Correct?

1. afternoon

2. morning

3. lunch

4. dinner

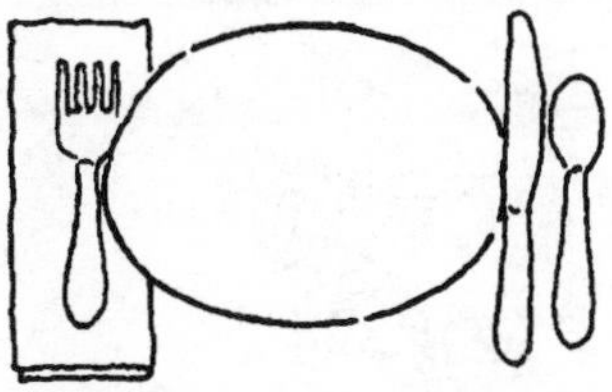  

5. sleep

 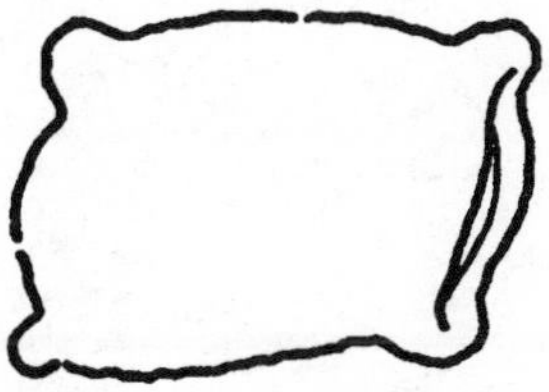 

Teacher Read the words aloud. Have students draw an X over the picture that does NOT make sense.

Score ______
(Top Score 5)

3 Build New Vocabulary

Favorite Foods

1. drink

2. eat

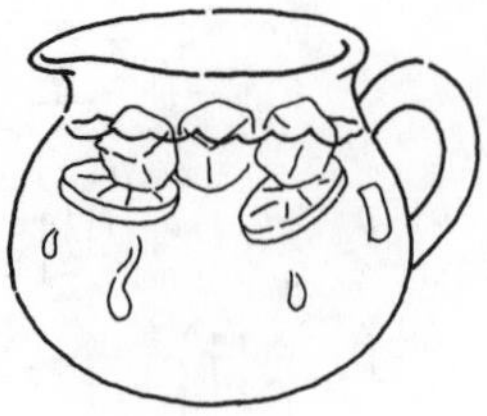

BREAD

3. lunch

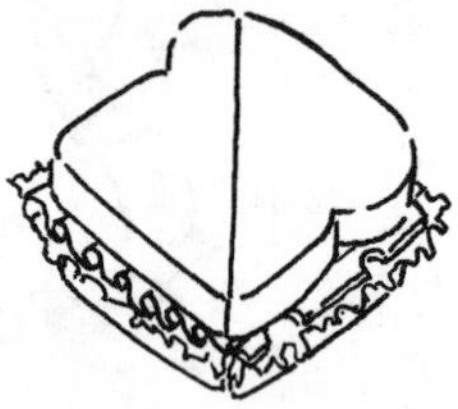
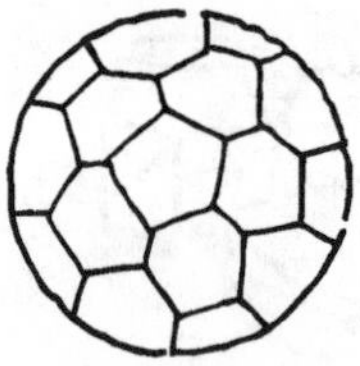

4. dinner

5. breakfast

Score ______
(Top Score 5)

Teacher Read each word aloud. Have students draw a circle around the picture that best relates to the word.

Vocabulary List		
1. wake	3. eat	7. wash
2. morning	4. drink	8. dinner
	5. lunch	9. sleep
	6. afternoon	10. night

4 Word Play

When Does It Happen?

1. morning

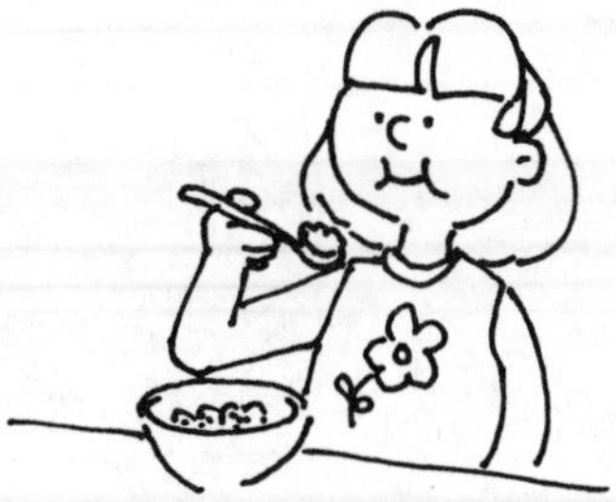

2. afternoon

ABC

3. night

Teacher Read each word aloud. Have students draw an X over the picture that does NOT relate to that time of the day.

Score ______
(Top Score 3)

Size and Shape

1 Word Meanings

Identifying Examples

1. big

2. little

3. tall

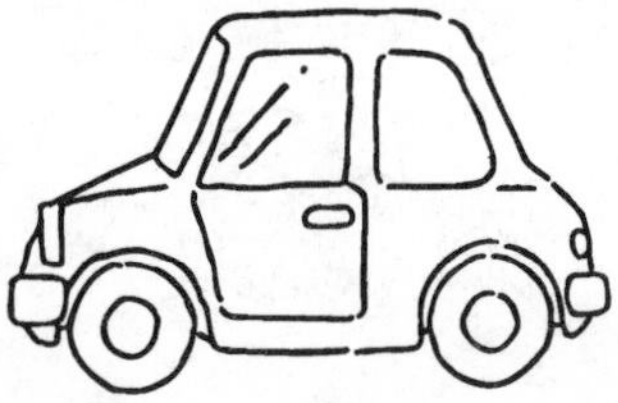

4. half

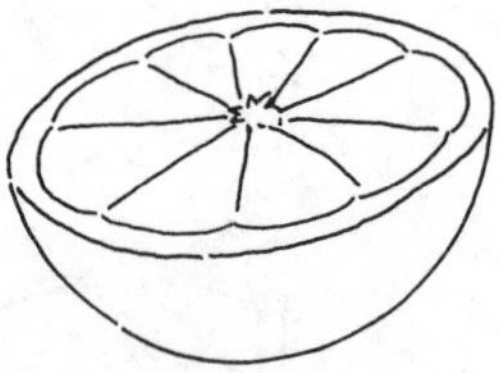
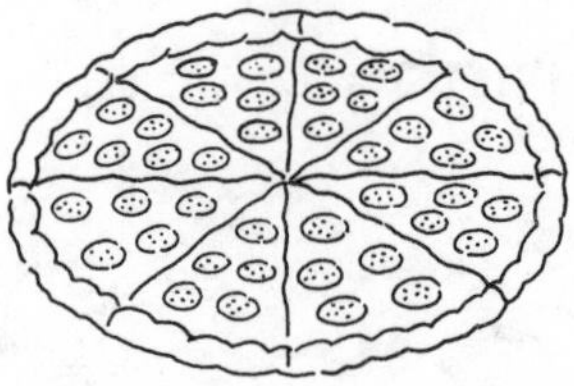

5. round

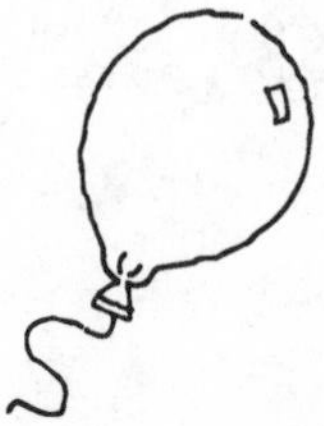

Score ______
(Top Score 5)

Teacher Read each word aloud. Have students draw an X over the picture that is NOT an example of the word.

Vocabulary List

1. all
2. little
3. big
4. full
5. long
6. round
7. small
8. short
9. tall
10. half

2 Reference Skills

Same and Opposite

1. little

A. 

2. big

B. 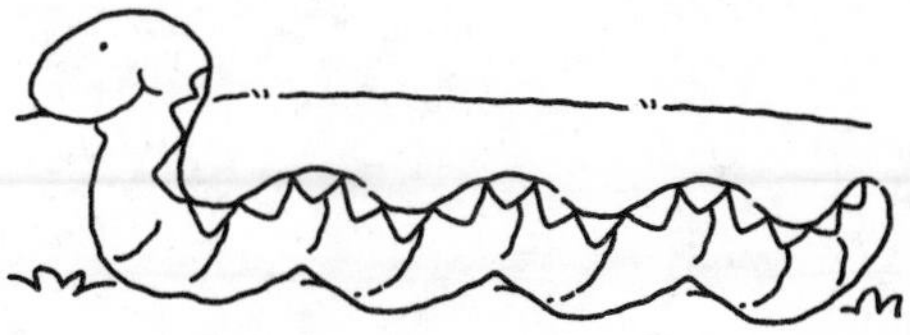

3. long

C. 

---

4. small

D. 

5. short

E. 

6. tall

F. 

Teacher Read the first set of words aloud. Have students draw a line from the word to the picture that best matches the meaning of the word. Read the second set of words aloud. Have students draw a line from the word to the picture that has the opposite meaning of the word.

Score ______
(Top Score 6)

3 Build New Vocabulary

Shapes That Describe

1. round

A.

2. oval

B.

THE
UGLY
DUCKLING

3. square

C.

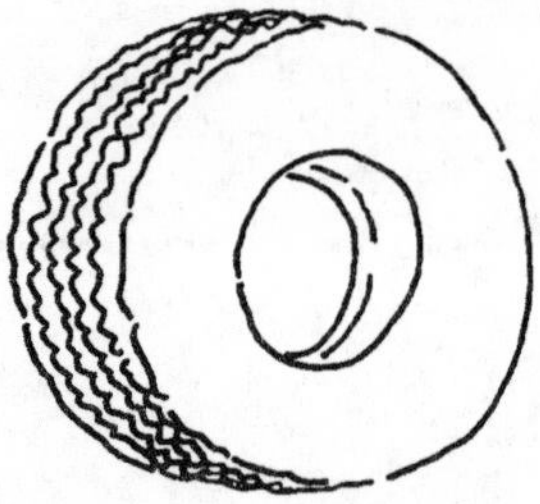

4. diamond

D.

A

5. rectangle

E.

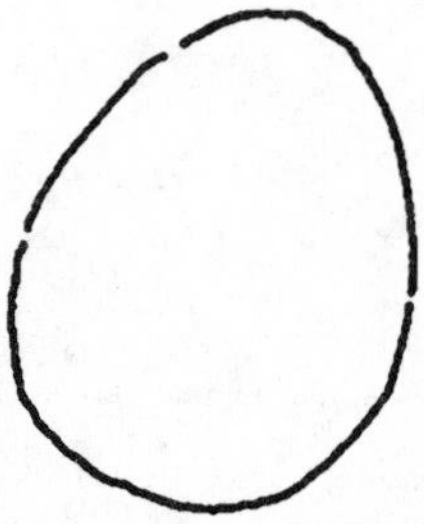

Score ______
(Top Score 5)

Teacher Read each word aloud. Have students draw a line from the word to the picture that best describes the word.

Vocabulary List		
1. all	3. big	7. small
2. little	4. full	8. short
	5. long	9. tall
	6. round	10. half

4 Word Play

How Does the Story Change?

1.

2.

3.

4.

5.

Teacher For each number, have students look closely at each pair of pictures. Instruct students to draw an X over the picture that does NOT make sense.

Score _____
(Top Score 5)

Vocabulary Review

1 Review Word Meanings

1. In the morning, I couldn't wait to jump out of bed.

2. In the morning, I couldn't wait to jump out of bed.

3. The night before, my mom and I had picked out my clothes for the day.

4. We placed them on the chair next to my bed.

5. So I picked up my things before I went downstairs to eat breakfast.

Score ______
(Top Score 5)

Teacher Read aloud the story on page 70 in the ***Teacher's Edition*** OR read the sentences above for each number. Tell students to draw a circle around the picture that best matches the underlined word.

2 Review Word Meanings

1. The kitchen smelled like warm maple syrup and pancakes.

GO TEAM

2. I asked for a full glass of orange juice to have with my two round pancakes.

3. I went into the bathroom to brush my teeth and wash my hands.

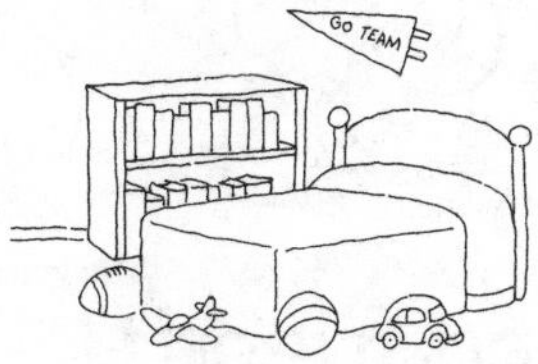
GO TEAM

4. Mom asked me if I knew Gina's address.

DAILY NEWS

321
Oak Street

Three
Little
Pigs

5. We were so happy to be going to the zoo together.

Teacher Read aloud the story on page 71 in the *Teacher's Edition* OR read the sentences above for each number. Tell students to draw a circle around the picture that best matches the underlined word.

Score ______
(Top Score 5)

3 Review Word Meanings

1. Gina and I like to play many of the same games.

2. Gina is a very kind person.

PEANUT BUTTER

3. She shared her new crayons with me.

SALE
$
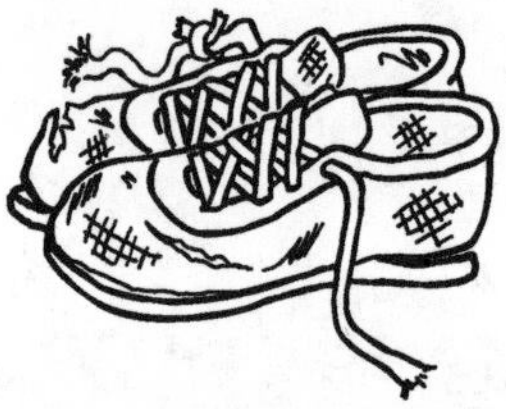

4. I am sad because I miss my old school and friends.

5. Gina asked to see the tall giraffes.

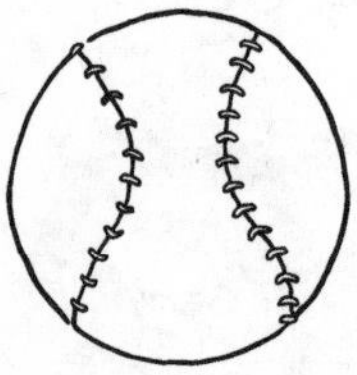

Score ______
(Top Score 5)

Teacher Read aloud the story on page 72 in the ***Teacher's Edition*** OR read the sentences above for each number. Tell students to draw a circle around the picture that best matches the underlined word.

4 Review Word Meanings

1. Gina and I ran to see the big elephants.

2. The small elephant was much bigger than we were!

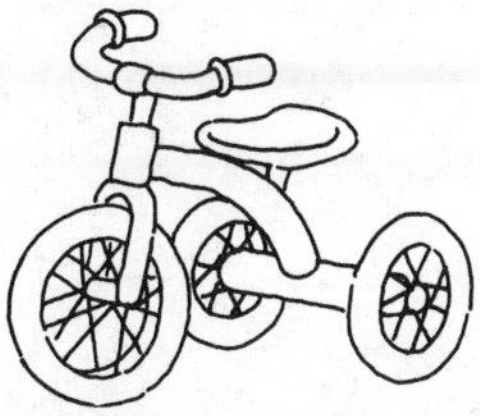

3. We stopped for a drink of water on our way to see the monkeys.

4. A monkey had a long tail wrapped around a tree branch.

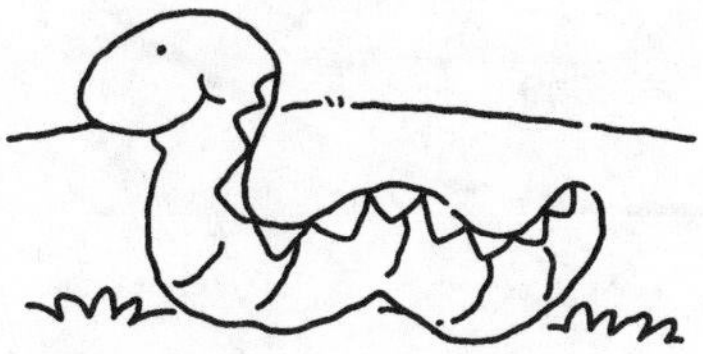
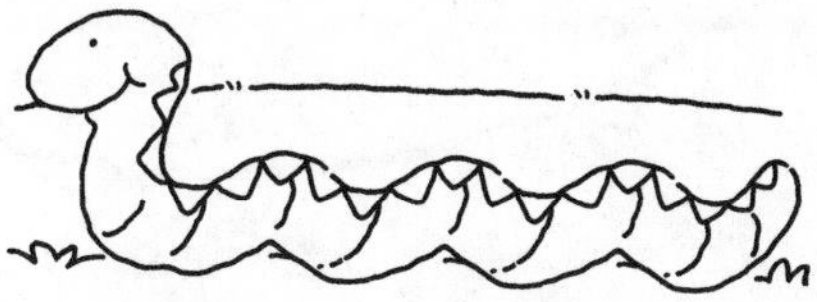

5. I placed the picture frame on the fireplace mantle.

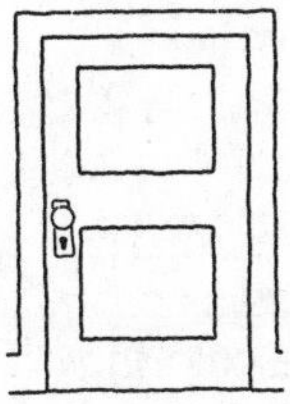

Teacher Read aloud the story on page 73 in the *Teacher's Edition* OR read the sentences above for each number. Tell students to draw a circle around the picture that best matches the underlined word.

Score ____
(Top Score 5)

"Wind" Vocabulary

1 Word Meanings

Venn Diagram

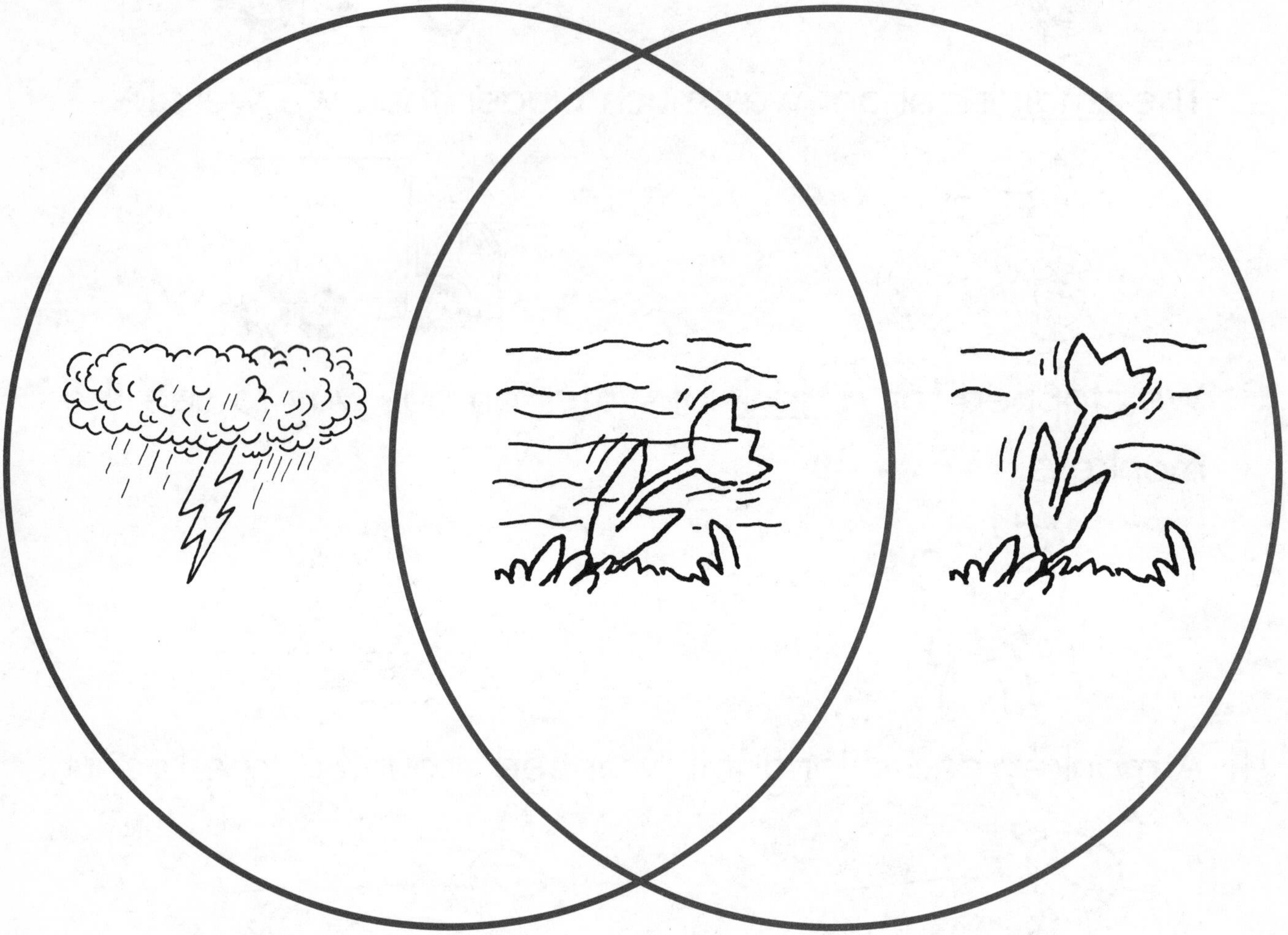

1. storm 2. blow 3. breeze

Teacher Each student will need a blue, red, and green crayon. Have students listen carefully as you read each word aloud. Have them color the part of the diagram that best shows the vocabulary word. Read each word below the diagram aloud. Check that students are coloring the correct section of the diagram (*storm*–blue; *blow*–red; *breeze*–green).

Score ______
(Top Score 3)

Vocabulary List
1. air
2. blustery
3. breeze
4. blow
5. whistle
6. storm
7. windmill
8. kite
9. strong
10. gust

2 Reference Skills

Alphabetical Order

1. blow	kite
2. whistle	gust
3. air	breeze
4. windmill	strong
5. storm	blustery

Teacher Read each pair of words aloud. Have students circle the first letter of each word in each pair. Then have them circle the one word in each pair that comes first alphabetically.

Score ______
(Top Score 5)

3 Build New Vocabulary

Adding -y

1. stormy

2. gusty

3. airy

4. blustery

5. breezy

Score ______
(Top Score 5)

Teacher Read each vocabulary word aloud. Have students trace the *-y* ending and repeat the new word with you.

Vocabulary List
1. air
2. blustery
3. breeze
4. blow
5. whistle
6. storm
7. windmill
8. kite
9. strong
10. gust

4 Word Play

Describing the Weather

1. My hat blew off in the ______________ wind.

strong   air

2. The ______________ was cold, so I put on my jacket.

air   windmill

3. I flew my kite in the ______________.

whistle   breeze

4. The trip to the zoo was canceled because of the ______________.

storm   blustery

5. To make the windmill work, the wind must ______________.

strong   blow

Teacher Read each incomplete sentence aloud. Read the two word choices below. Have students circle the vocabulary word that best completes the sentence.

Score ______
(Top Score 5)

"Stick to It" Vocabulary

1 Word Meanings

Learn By Doing

1. The first person to cross the finish line will ______________ the race.

   can   win

2. Your ______________ should be to always do your best.

   goal   reach

3. If you do not win the first time, ______________ again.

   wish   try

4. When you are standing in line, you must ______________ your turn.

   keep   wait

5. Will you toss the beanbag, or will you run the ______________?

   race   brave

Score _____
(Top Score 5)

Teacher Read each incomplete sentence aloud. Have students listen to the two answer choices and then circle the vocabulary word that best completes the sentence.

Vocabulary List

1. try
2. win
3. wish
4. reach
5. race
6. wait
7. brave
8. keep
9. can
10. goal

2 Reference Skills

Which Word Works?

1. I ________________ tie my shoes.

brave can

2. I made a ________________ for a new bicycle.

wait wish

3. I wanted to ________________ playing on the playground.

keep reach

4. She kicked the soccer ball into the ________________.

goal try

5. Did he ________________ the race?

goal win

Teacher Read each incomplete sentence aloud. Read the two word choices below. Have students circle the vocabulary word that completes the sentence.

Score ____
(Top Score 5)

3 Build New Vocabulary

Word Relationships

1. win

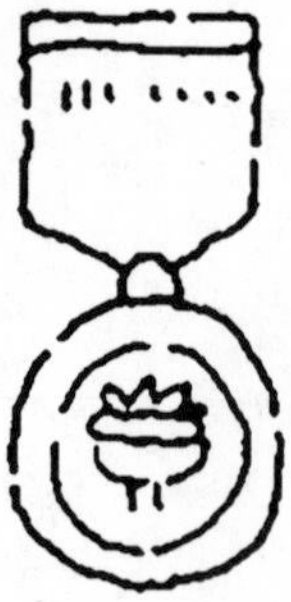

1ST

2. race

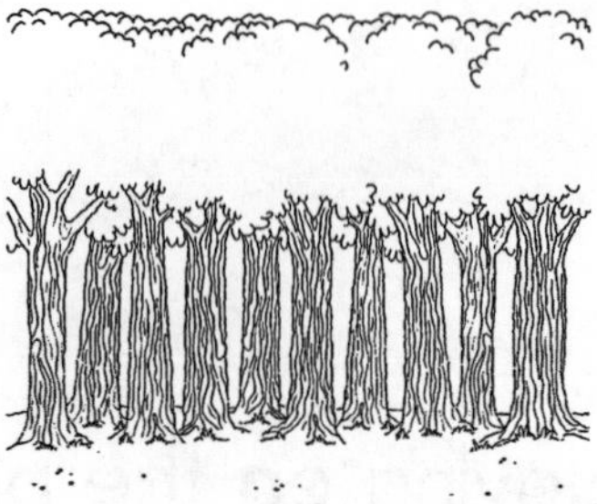

3. brave

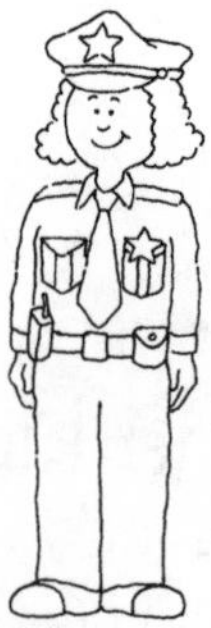

4. goal

FINISH LINE

Score ______
(Top Score 4)

Teacher Read each word aloud. Have students look closely at each picture. Tell them to draw an X over the picture that does not belong with the word.

Vocabulary List
1. try
2. win
3. wish
4. reach
5. race
6. wait
7. brave
8. keep
9. can
10. goal

4 Word Play

I Can Do It!

1. I can put on my ______________.

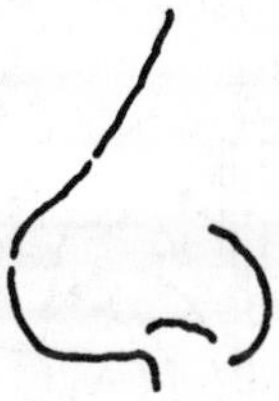

2. I can brush my ______________.

3. I can pour my ______________.

4. I can kick the ______________.

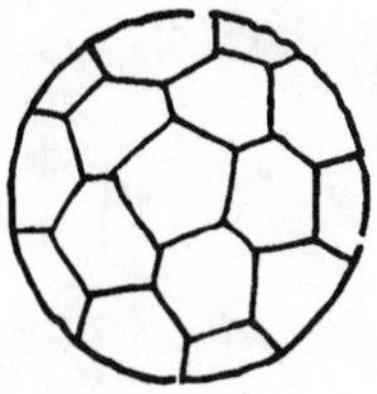

S

5. I can fly the ______________.

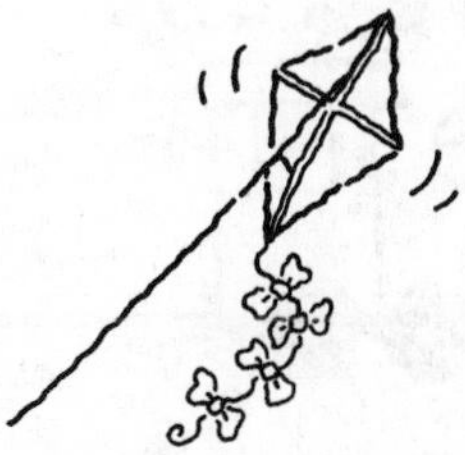

Teacher Read each incomplete sentence aloud. Have students look closely at each picture below. Tell them to draw a circle around the picture that best completes the sentence.

Score ______
(Top Score 5)

Sound Vocabulary

1 Word Meanings

Make a Noise!

1. clap

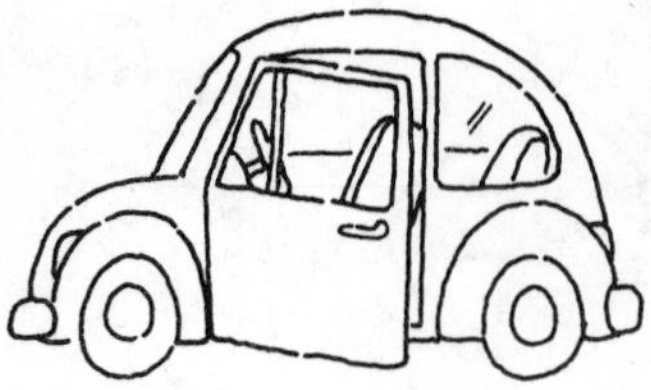

2. honk

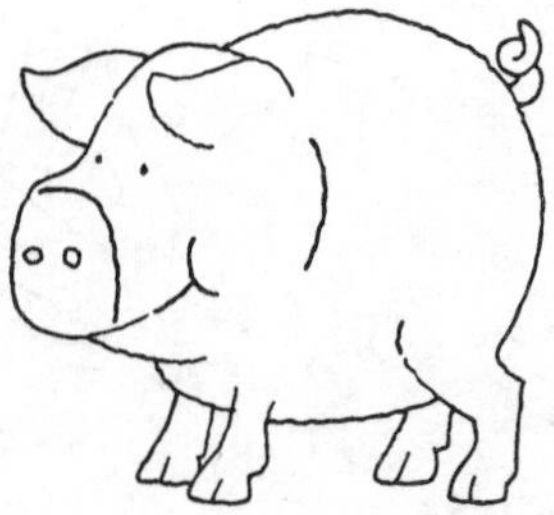

3. bang

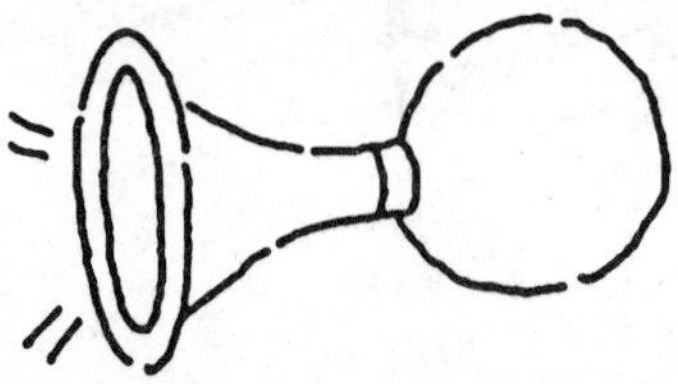

4. rattle

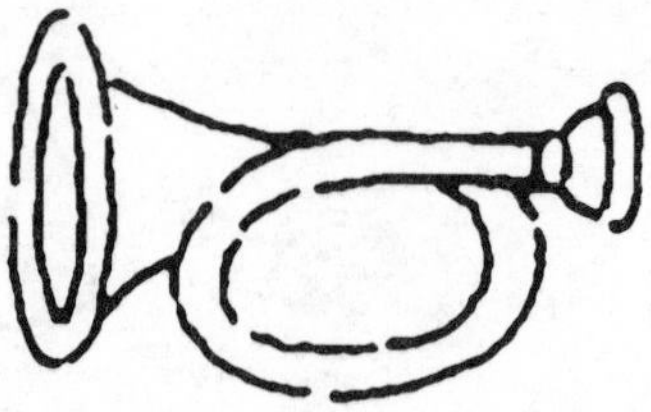

5. meow

Score ______
(Top Score 5)

Teacher Read each sound word aloud. Have students look closely at the three pictures beneath the word. Tell them to draw a circle around the picture that best matches the sound word.

Vocabulary List

1. clap	3. bang	7. call
2. honk	4. meow	8. tell
	5. rattle	9. say
	6. buzz	10. hear

2 Reference Skills

Picture Dictionary

1. bang

2. buzz

3. hear

4. honk

5. say

A. 

B. 

C. 

D. 

E. 

Teacher Read each word aloud. Have students draw a line from each word to the picture that it matches.

Score ______
(Top Score 5)

3 Build New Vocabulary

More Sound Words

1. ticktock
2. boom
3. flip-flop
4. zoom
5. slam

A.

B.

11 12 1
10 2
9 3
8 4
7 6 5

C.

D.

E.

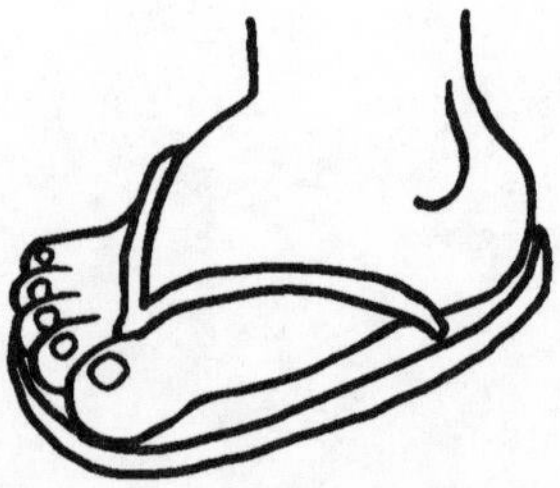

Score ______
(Top Score 5)

Teacher Read each word aloud. Have students draw a line from each word to the picture that it matches.

Vocabulary List		
1. clap	3. bang	7. call
2. honk	4. meow	8. tell
	5. rattle	9. say
	6. buzz	10. hear

4 Word Play

Making Sounds

1.  howl bang

2.  clap honk

3.  rattle buzz

4.  clap call

5.  meow rattle

Teacher Have students look closely at each picture. Read the two word choices aloud. Tell students to draw a circle around the word that best describes the sound that the picture would make.

Score _____
(Top Score 5)

"Show and Tell" Vocabulary

1 Word Meanings

Describing What You See

1. open

A. 

2. close

B. 

3. picture

C. 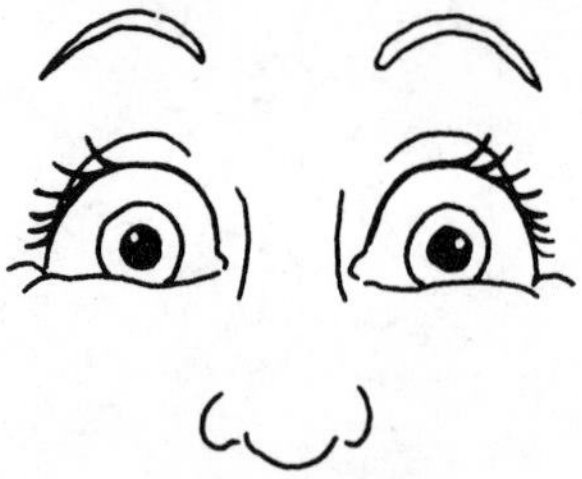

4. paint

D. 
GARAGE
SALE

5. poster

E. 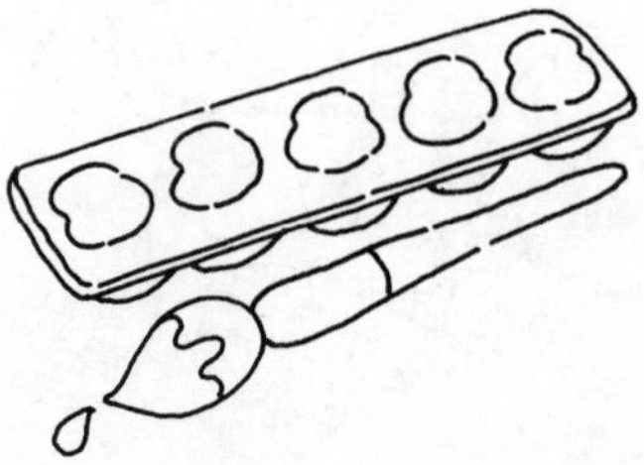

Score ______
(Top Score 5)

Teacher Read each word aloud. Have students look closely at each picture. Instruct them to draw a line from the word to the picture that best matches it.

Vocabulary List		
1. open	3. see	7. idea
2. close	4. look	8. picture
	5. pretty	9. paint
	6. color	10. poster

2 Reference Skills

Alphabetical Order

a b c d e f g h i j k l m
n o p q r s t u v w x y z

______ idea

______ color

______ pretty

______ close

______ look

Teacher Read each word aloud. Have students place the words in alphabetical order. Tell them to write the number 1 next to the word that comes first, the number 2 next to the word that comes second, and so on.

Score ______
(Top Score 5)

3 Build New Vocabulary

Open and Close

1. 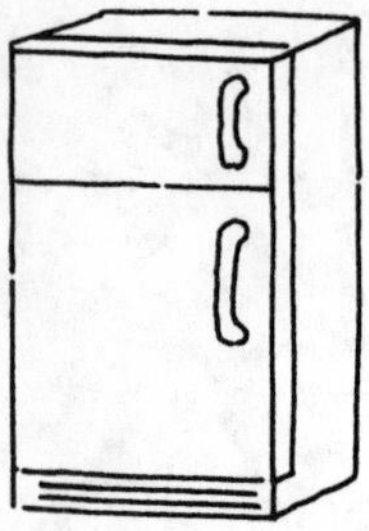 open close

2. 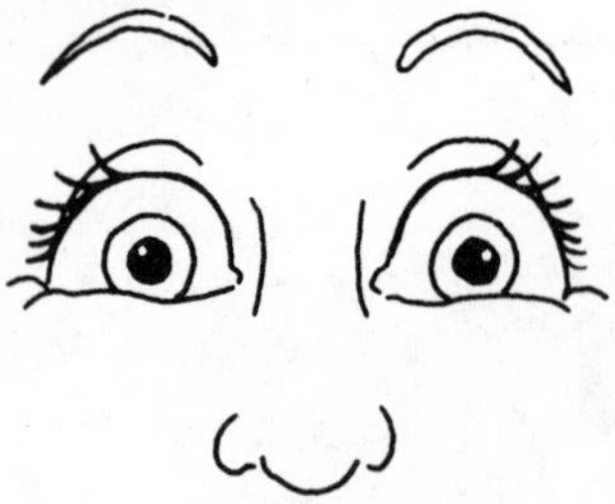 open close

3.  open close

4. 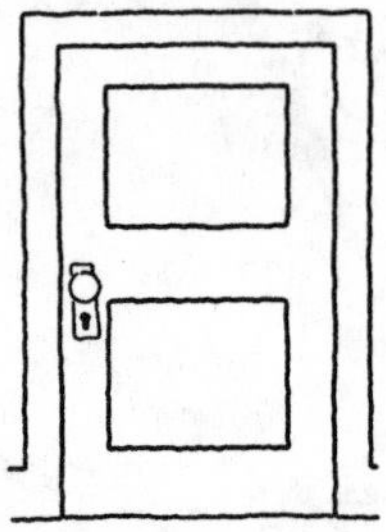 open close

5.  open close

Score _____
(Top Score 5)

Teacher Have students look closely at each picture. If the picture is an example of an open object, tell students to circle the word *open*. If the picture is an example of a closed object, tell students to circle the word *close*.

Vocabulary List		
1. open	3. see	7. idea
2. close	4. look	8. picture
	5. pretty	9. paint
	6. color	10. poster

4 Word Play

I Spy . . .

1. When we go to the zoo, we like to ______________ at the monkeys.

   look pretty

2. Please ______________ the door.

   idea open

3. She had to ______________ her eyes to sleep.

   close paint

4. I can ______________ the ducks in the pond.

   close see

5. He loves to ______________ with his crayons.

   color poster

Teacher Read each incomplete sentence aloud. Have students look closely at the words below. Tell them to draw a circle around the vocabulary word that best completes the sentence.

Score ______
(Top Score 5)

Vocabulary for Touch

1 Word Meanings

Feel the Opposites

1. cold

2. wet

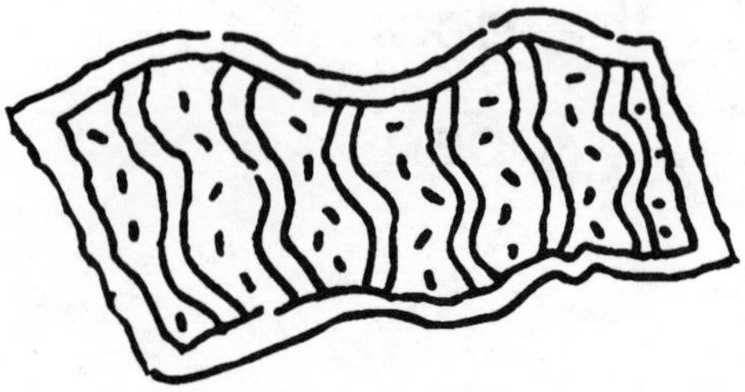

3. hard

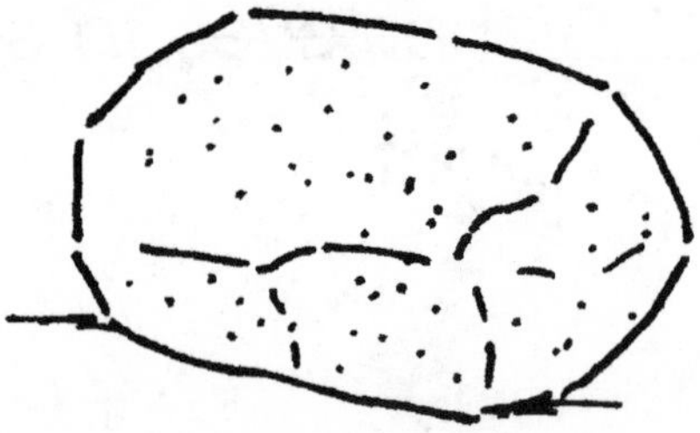
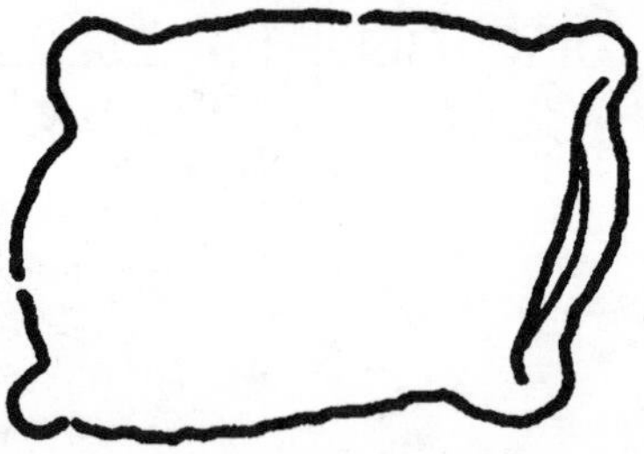

4. smooth

5. hot

Score ______
(Top Score 5)

Teacher Read each word aloud. Have students look closely at the two pictures beneath each word. Tell them to draw an X over the picture that represents the opposite of the word.

Vocabulary List

1. cold
2. cool
3. warm
4. hot
5. wet
6. dry
7. soft
8. hard
9. smooth
10. bumpy

2 Reference Skills

Cold–Cool–Warm–Hot

1. Don't touch the ________________ stove!

   warm hot

2. Let's go ________________ our hands by the campfire.

   cool warm

3. When it's hot out, I like to ________________ off in the pool.

   cool cold

4. Add ice to make a drink ________________.

   cold hot

5. The sun is ________________.

   cool hot

Teacher Read each incomplete sentence aloud. Read each word choice aloud. Tell students to draw a circle around the word that best completes each sentence.

Score ______
(Top Score 5)

3 Build New Vocabulary

Sticky, Prickly, Squishy

1. soft

A.

2. hard

B.

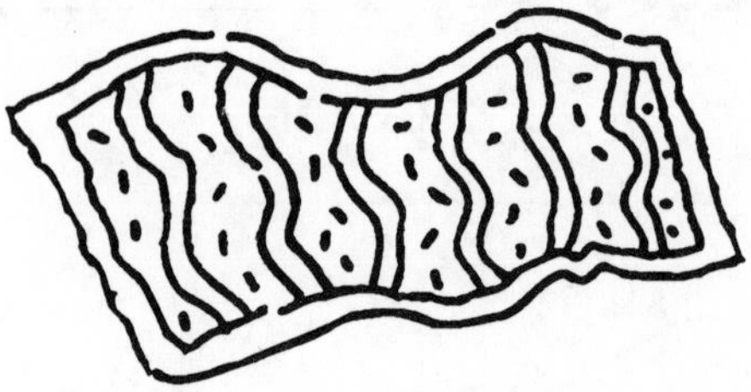

3. smooth

C.

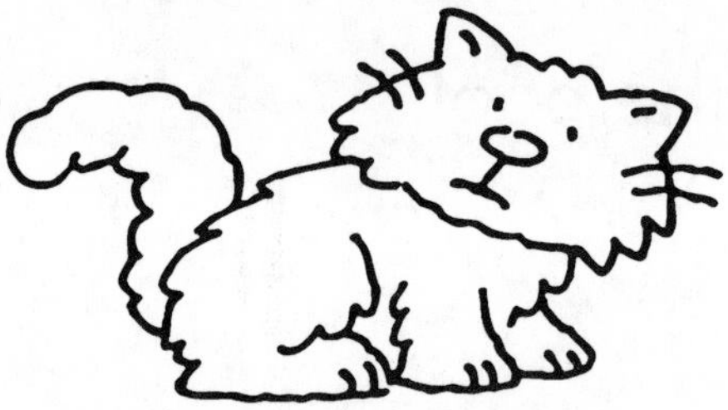

4. bumpy

D.

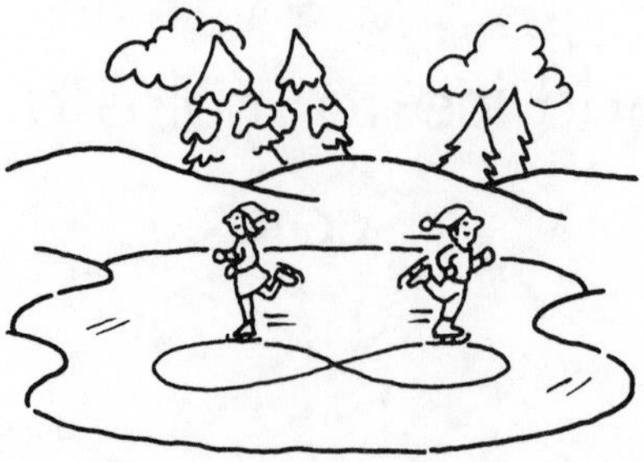

5. dry

E.

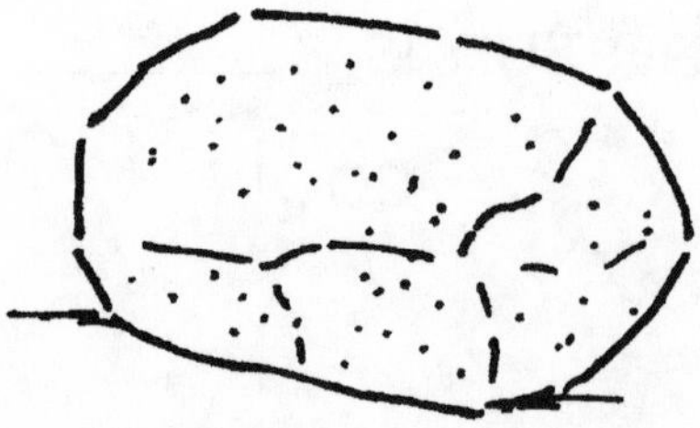

Score _____
(Top Score 5)

Teacher Read each word aloud. Have students look closely at each picture. Tell them to draw a line from the word to the picture that best matches it.

Vocabulary List		
1. cold	3. warm	7. soft
2. cool	4. hot	8. hard
	5. wet	9. smooth
	6. dry	10. bumpy

4 Word Play

You're Getting Warmer ...

1. I wear mittens to keep my hands ______________.

   warm cool

2. The kitten's fur is ______________.

   hard soft

3. I drank a ______________ glass of water with ice cubes.

   cold hot

4. The ground was ______________ after the rainstorm.

   dry wet

5. The children skated on the ______________, icy surface of the pond.

   smooth bumpy

Teacher Read each incomplete sentence aloud. Tell students to draw a circle around the word that best completes the sentence.

Score ______
(Top Score 5)

Vocabulary Review

1 Review Word Meanings

1. The picture showed a group of children having fun.

Three
Little
Pigs

2. The clouds darken and the breeze blows harder.

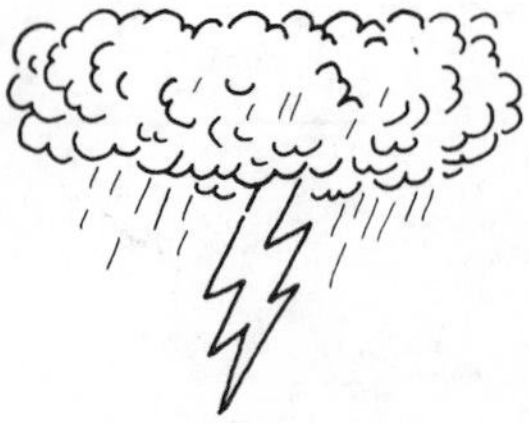

3. I am getting cold.

BUMP

4. Someone calls for the race to start.

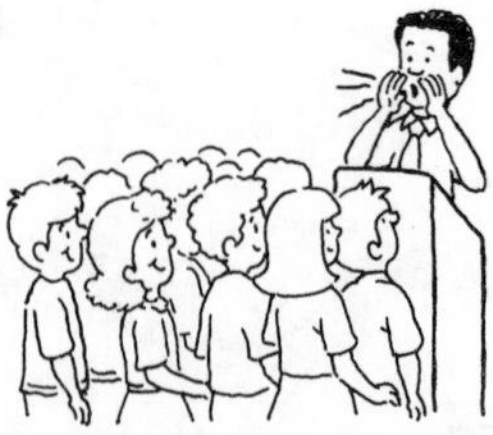

5. He is wearing a jacket the color of a bright pumpkin.

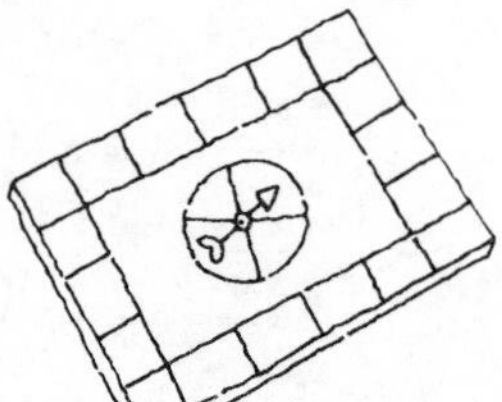

Score ______
(Top Score 5)

Teacher Read the story on page 94 in the ***Teacher's Edition*** OR read the numbered sentences above. Tell students to draw a circle around the picture that best matches the underlined word.

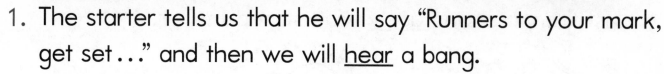

2 Review Word Meanings

1. The starter tells us that he will say "Runners to your mark, get set..." and then we will hear a bang.

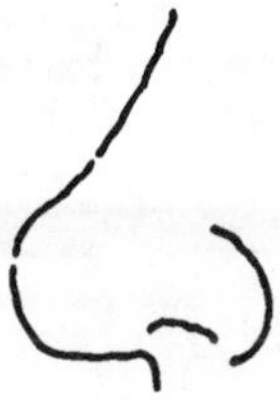
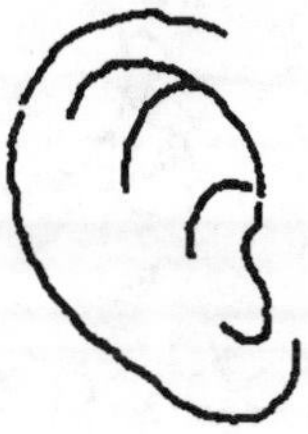
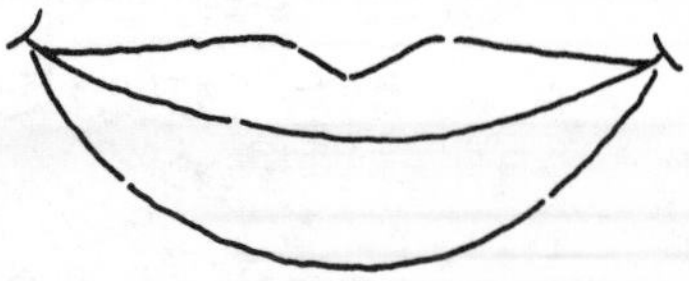

2. I look into the crowd.

3. My grandmother waves and claps her hands for me.

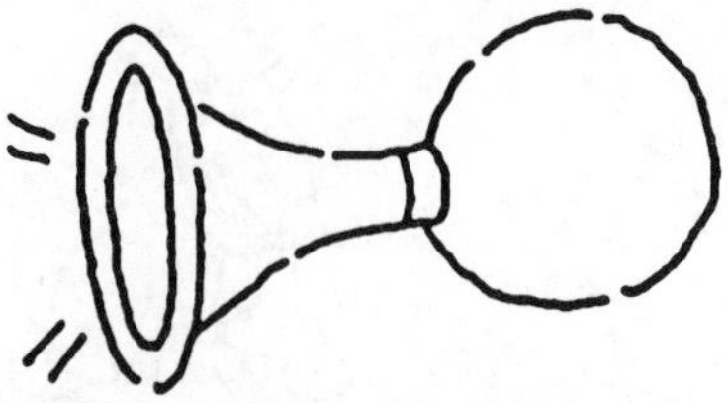

4. The noise quiets to a weak buzz.

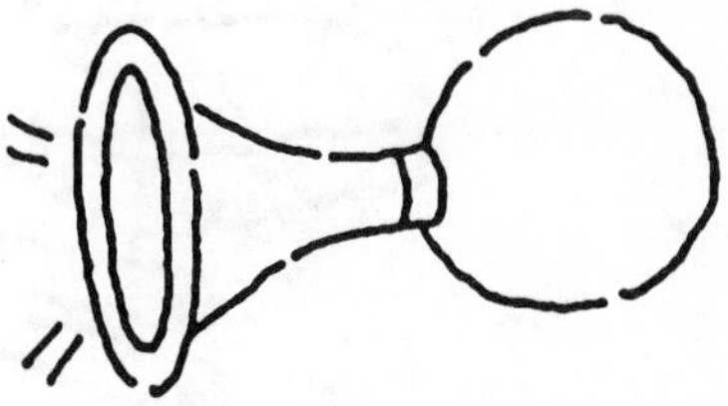

5. We heard the whistles blow.

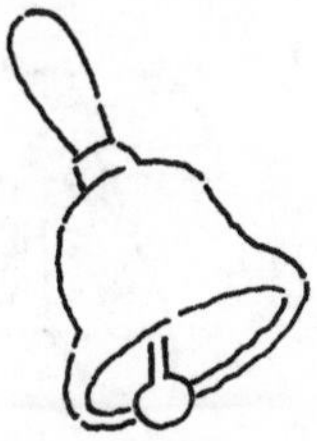
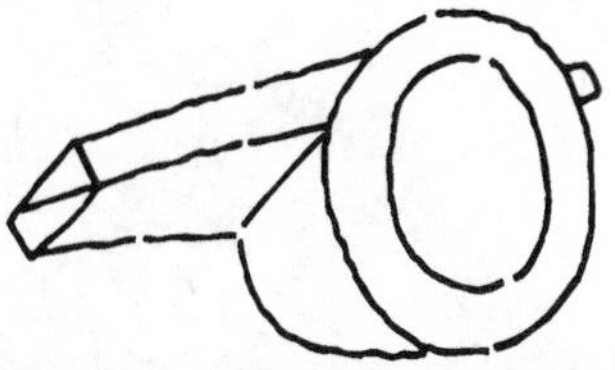

Teacher Read the story on page 95 in the ***Teacher's Edition*** OR read the numbered sentences above. Tell students to draw a circle around the picture that best matches the underlined word.

Score ______
(Top Score 5)

3 Review Word Meanings

1. Just then, a strong gusty wind stirred the air.

2. I closed my eyes and took a deep breath.

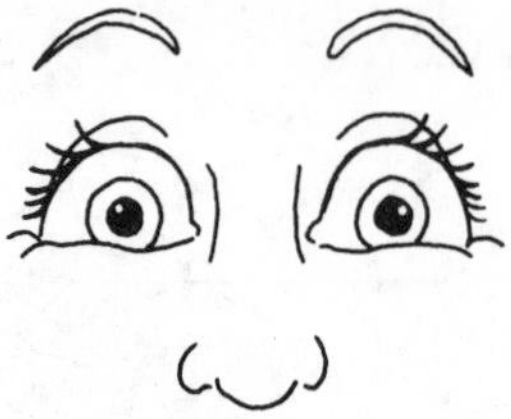
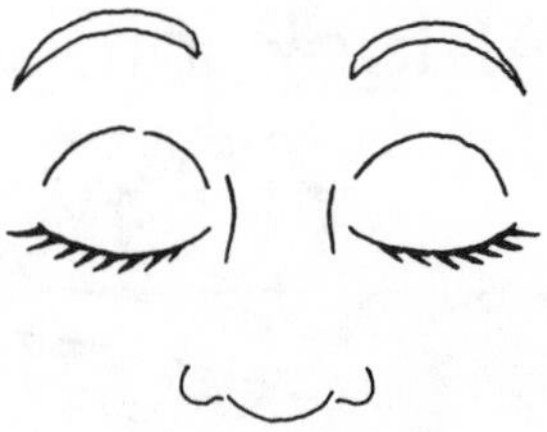

3. First we ran on the hard track, but then we ran on the soft grass.

4. The colors reminded me of watercolor paints.

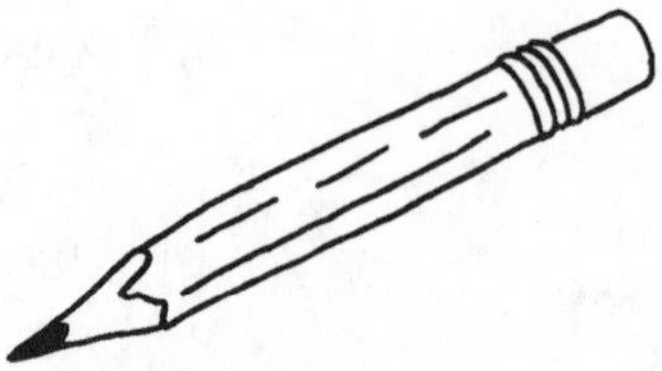
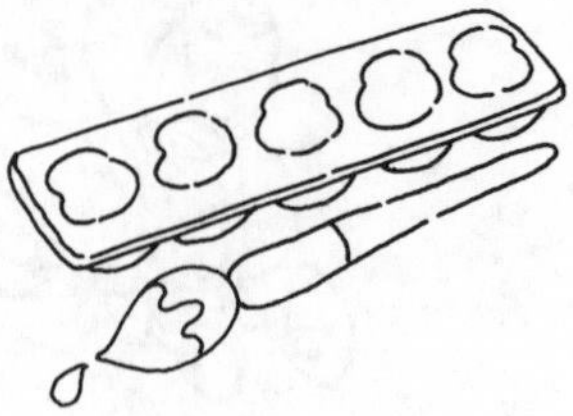

5. I was warm at first, but then I felt hot.

Score ______
(Top Score 5)

Teacher Read the story on page 96 in the ***Teacher's Edition*** OR read the numbered sentences above. Tell students to draw a circle around the picture that best matches the underlined word.

4 Review Word Meanings

1. My grandmother thought I was very brave.

2. She said it wasn't important to win the race, but to reach my goal of finishing the race.

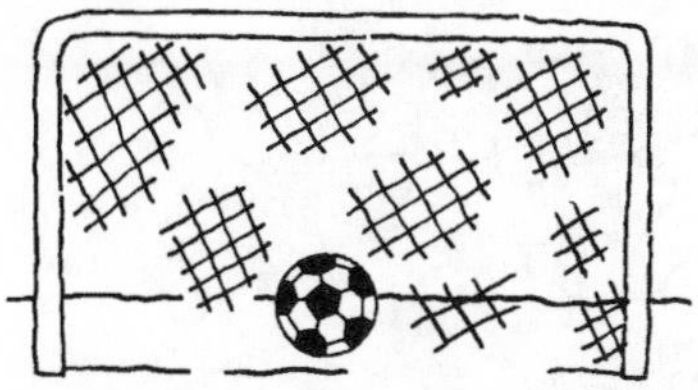

FINISH LINE

3. I heard people honking their horns.

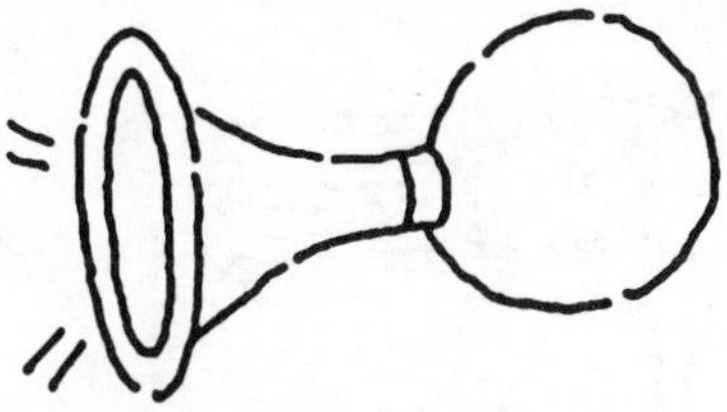

4. I was hot and sweaty, and my forehead was wet.

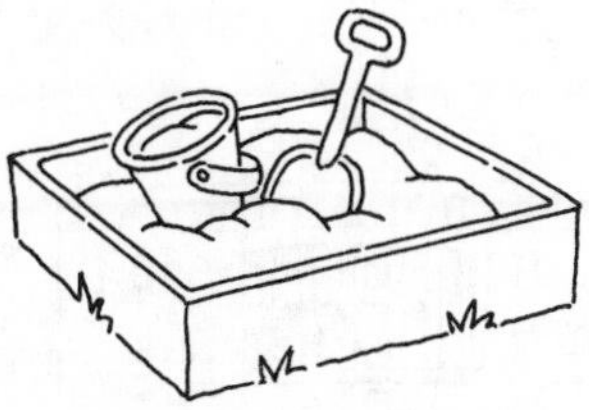

5. My grandmother smiled proudly and handed me a dry towel.

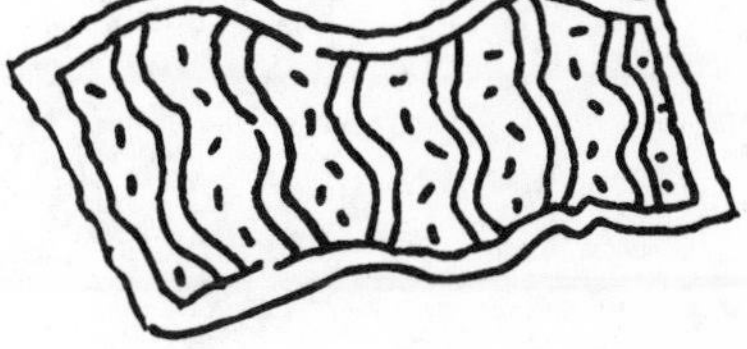

Teacher Read the story on page 97 in the ***Teacher's Edition*** OR read the numbered sentences above. Tell students to draw a circle around the picture that best matches the underlined word.

Score ______
(Top Score 5)

Unit 5 Lesson 25

"Red, White, and Blue" Vocabulary

1 Word Meanings

Patriotic Meanings

1. flag

2. United States

3. president

4. Americans

5. state

A. 

B. 

C. 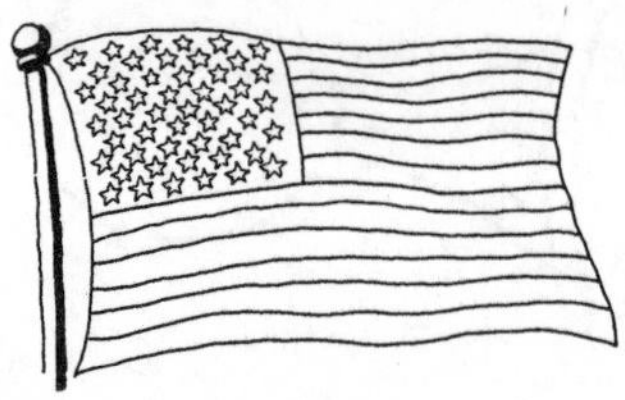

D. 

E. 

Score ______
(Top Score 5)

Teacher Read each numbered word aloud. Have students draw a line from the vocabulary word to the picture it matches.

Vocabulary List
1. American
2. state
3. United States
4. country
5. president
6. leader
7. land
8. flag
9. we
10. our

2 Reference Skills

Picture Dictionary

1. flag

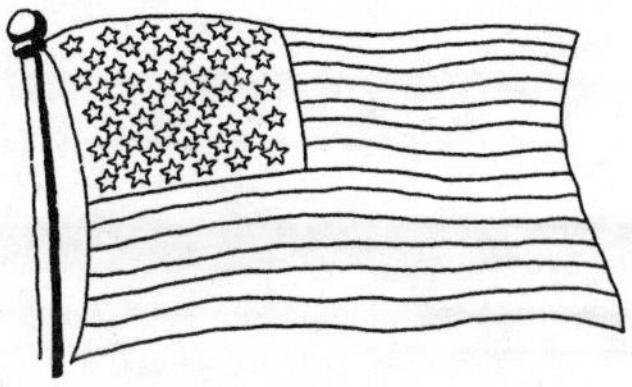

2. leader

3. land

4. state

MILK

5. country

Teacher Read each numbered word aloud. Have students look closely at each word and draw a circle around the picture that it best matches.

Score _____
(Top Score 5)

3 Build New Vocabulary

Proper Nouns

1. I am an American.

2. I live in the United States.

3. She lives in the state of Texas.

4. The president lives in the White House.

5. We walked to the top of the Statue of Liberty.

Score ______
(Top Score 5)

Teacher Have students follow along as you read each sentence aloud. Tell them to identify and circle the proper noun in each sentence by looking for the capital letter.

Vocabulary List
1. American
2. state
3. United States
4. country
5. president
6. leader
7. land
8. flag
9. we
10. our

4 Word Play

World Neighbors

Canada
United States
Mexico

Teacher As you read each name aloud, have students color each country a different color. Check to see that the students color the countries in the order that you read them.

Score ______
(Top Score 3)

"Teamwork" Vocabulary

1 Word Meanings

Human Knot

1. Can you ________ the wagon?

   pull everyone

2. He wanted to ________ the door open.

   group push

3. We built the tower of blocks ________.

   help together

4. Please ________ her the present.

   give join

5. She wore a scarf ________ her coat.

   let with

Score ____
(Top Score 5)

Teacher Read each incomplete sentence aloud. Read each word choice and have students circle the vocabulary word that best fits the sentence.

Vocabulary List
1. give
2. together
3. pull
4. push
5. let
6. with
7. join
8. group
9. help
10. everyone

2 Reference Skills

Body Language

1. pull

A.

2. push

B.

3. help

C.

4. together

D.

5. give

E.

Teacher Read each numbered word aloud. Have students look closely at each picture. Tell them to draw a line from the word to the picture that it best matches.

Score ______
(Top Score 5)

3 Build New Vocabulary

Groups

1.

2.

3.

4.

5.

Score ______
(Top Score 5)

Teacher For each numbered pair, have students circle the picture that best represents a group.

Vocabulary List
1. give
2. together
3. pull
4. push
5. let
6. with
7. join
8. group
9. help
10. everyone

4 Word Play

Teamwork

1.

2.

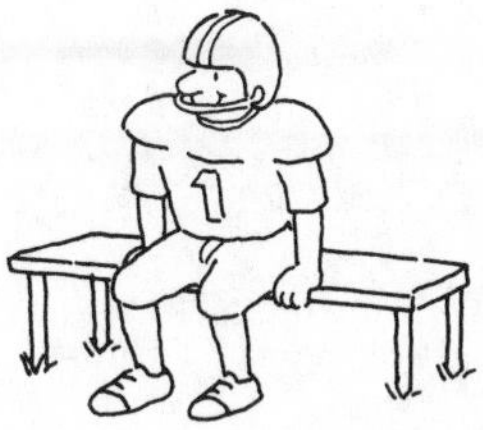

3.

4.

5.

Teacher Tell students to look closely at the pictures. Have them draw a circle around the picture that is an example of teamwork.

Score ______
(Top Score 5)

Compound Words

1 Word Meanings

Two Animals or One?

1. cowbell

A. 

2. anthill

B. 

3. goldfish

C. 

4. grasshopper

D. 

5. beehive

E. 

Score _____
(Top Score 5)

Teacher Read each vocabulary word aloud. Have students draw a line from the word to the picture that it best matches.

Vocabulary List
1. birdbath
2. bulldog
3. catfish
4. cowbell
5. birdhouse
6. firefly
7. beehive
8. anthill
9. goldfish
10. grasshopper

2 Reference Skills

Picture Equations

1. birdbath

A. 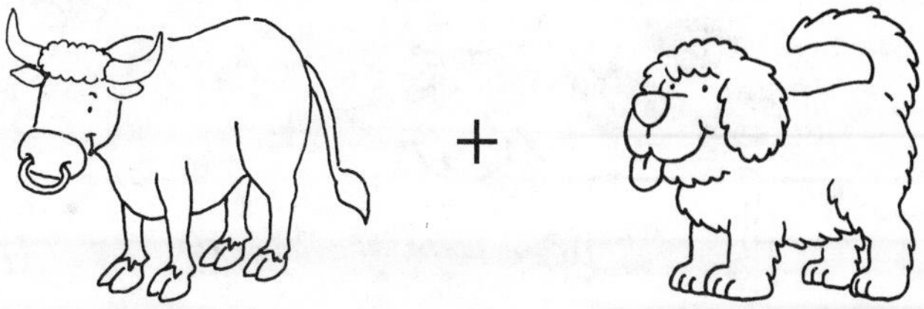

2. bulldog

B. 

3. birdhouse

C. 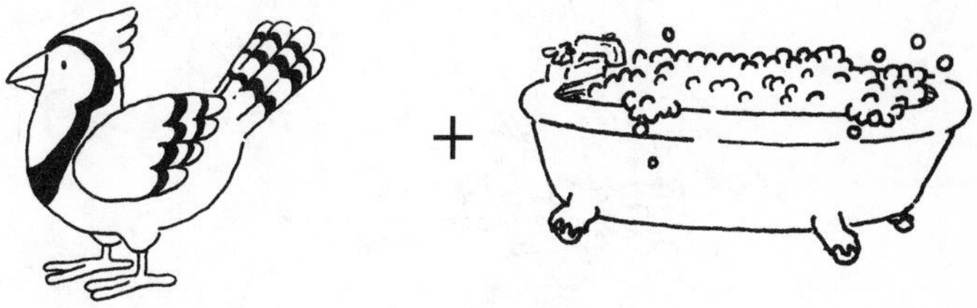

4. firefly

D. 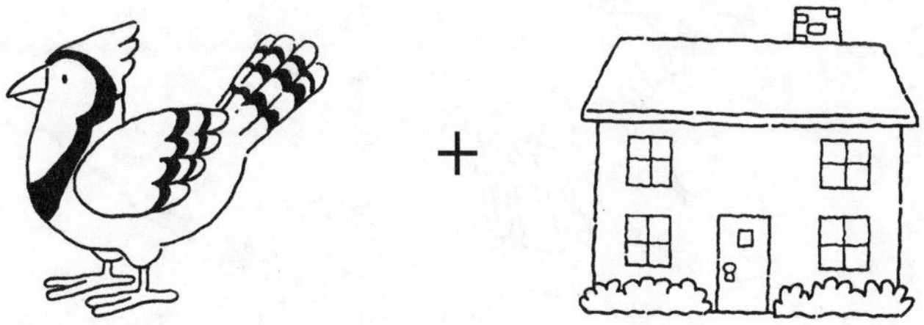

5. catfish

E. 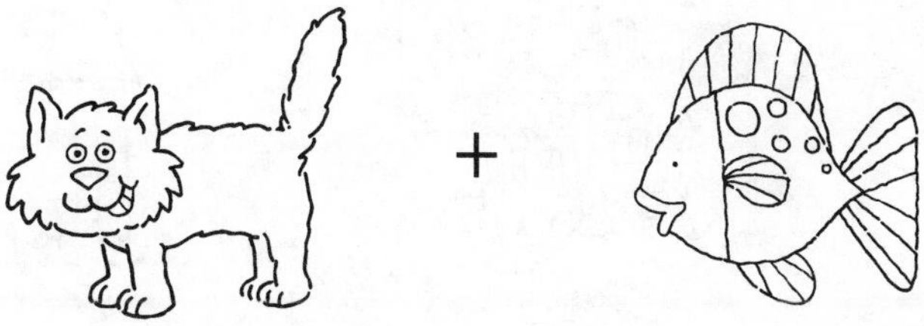

Teacher Read each compound word aloud. Tell students to look closely at the picture equations. Have them draw a line from the compound word to the picture equation that it matches.

Score ______
(Top Score 5)

3 Build New Vocabulary

More Compound Words

1.  + 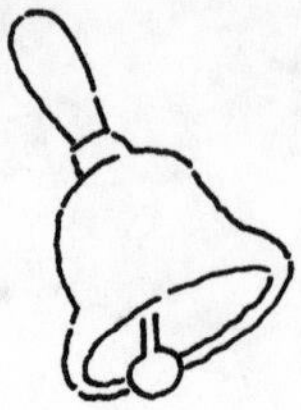 =

cowbell

butterfly

2.  +  =

catfish

goldfish

3.  + 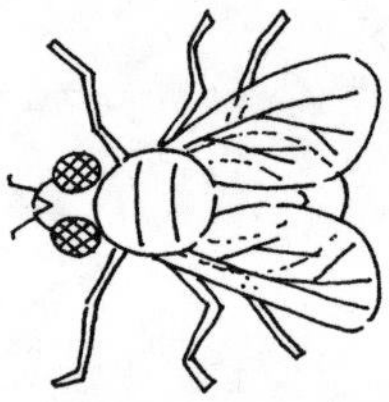 =

firefly

housefly

4.  +  =

earring

anthill

5. 
SCHOOL
\+  =

schoolhouse

housefly

Score ______
(Top Score 5)

Teacher Read each word choice aloud. Tell students to look at each set of pictures. Have them draw a circle around the compound word that best matches each set.

Vocabulary List
1. birdbath
2. bulldog
3. catfish
4. cowbell
5. birdhouse
6. firefly
7. beehive
8. anthill
9. goldfish
10. grasshopper

4 Word Play

Silly Words

1. goldfish

2. grasshopper

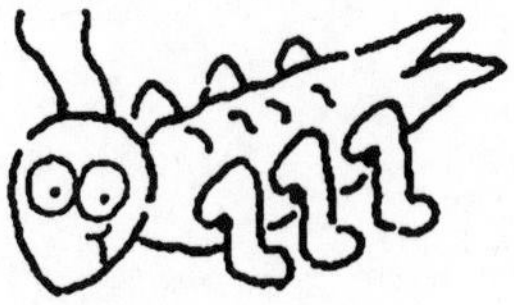

3. birdbath

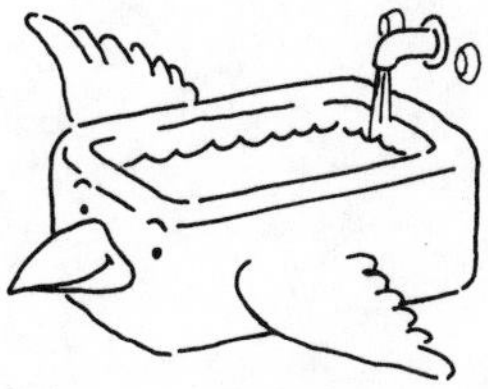

4. firefly

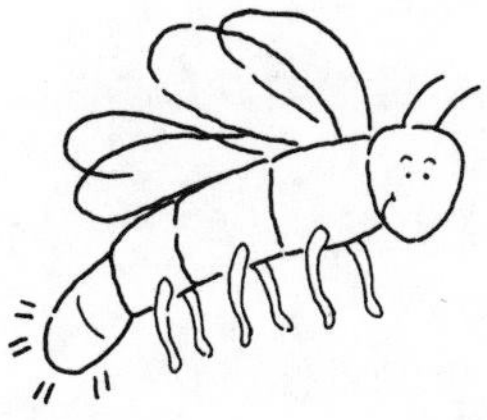

5. birdhouse

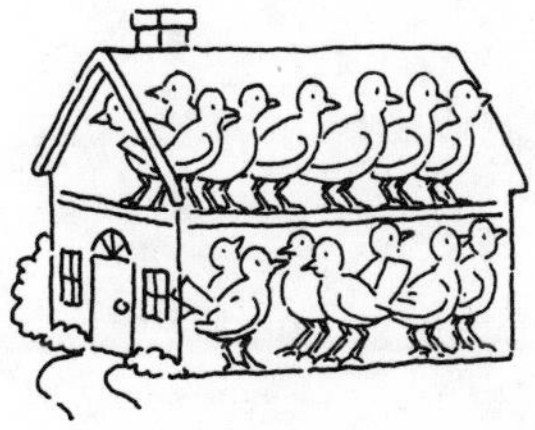

Teacher Read each word aloud. Have students look closely at each set of pictures. Tell them to draw an X over the silly picture.

Score ____
(Top Score 5)

"Make It-Fix It" Vocabulary

1 Word Meanings

Word Relationships

1. hammer

2. nail

3. glue

4. brick

5. tools

A.

B.

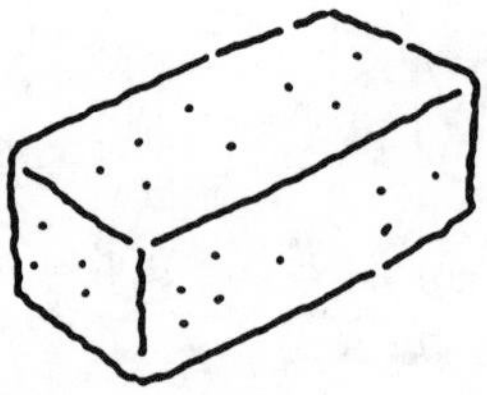

C.

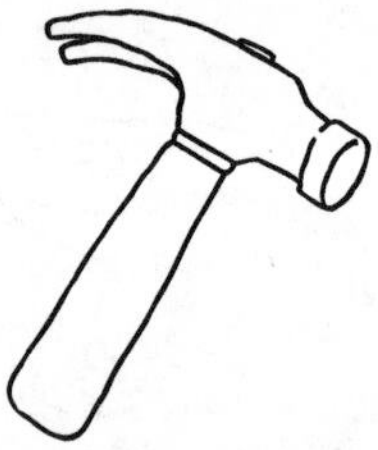

D.

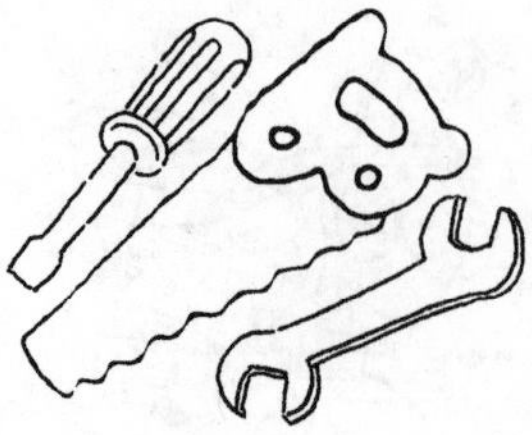

E.

Score _____
(Top Score 5)

Teacher Read each numbered word aloud. Have students draw a line from the vocabulary word to its corresponding picture.

Vocabulary List
1. use
2. build
3. fit
4. tight
5. hammer
6. nail
7. brick
8. fix
9. glue
10. tools

2 Reference Skills

Glue: Noun or Verb?

1. She glued the puzzle together.

GLUE

2. He used a bottle of glue in art class.

GLUE

3. Can you fix this with a bottle of glue?

GLUE

4. Mom glued the toy airplane together.

GLUE

5. We mixed paint with glue to make a picture.

GLUE

Teacher Explain that the bottle of glue represents the noun form of *glue,* and the student using the glue represents the verb form of *glue.* Read each sentence aloud. Have students draw a circle around the picture that represents how *glue* is being used in the sentence.

Score ______
(Top Score 5)

3 Build New Vocabulary

Word Association: Tools

1. nail

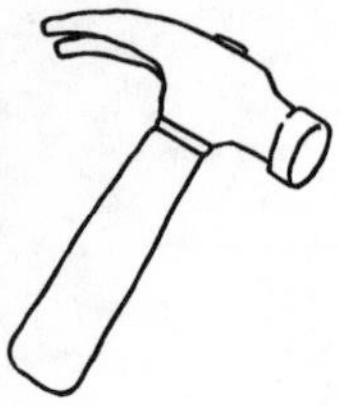
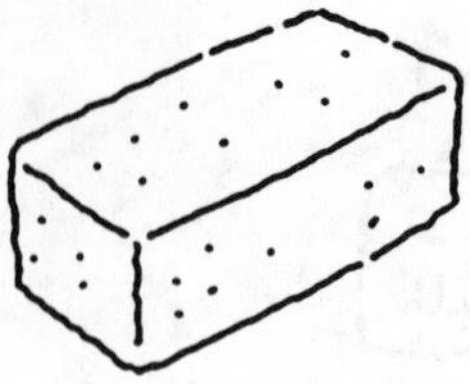

2. screw

3. shovel

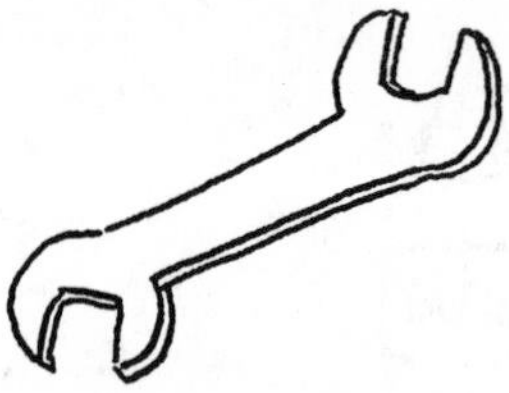

4. saw

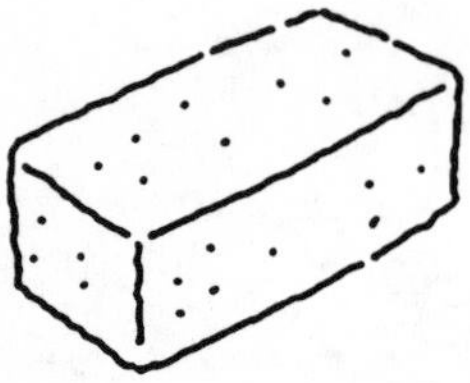
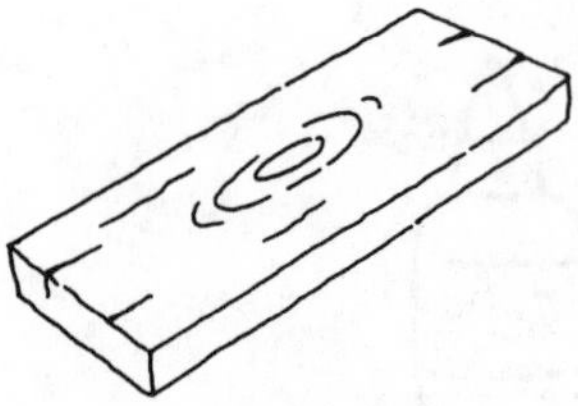

5. scissors

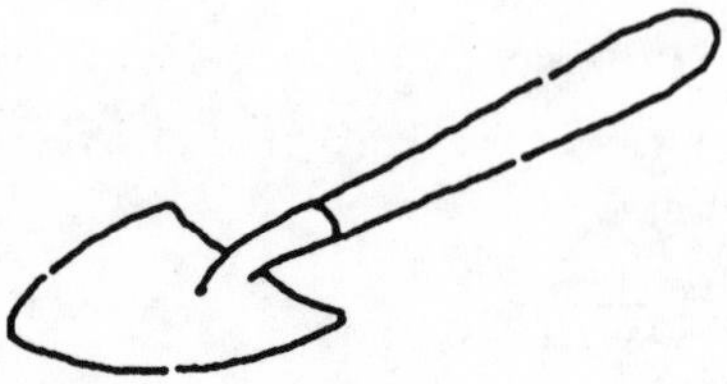
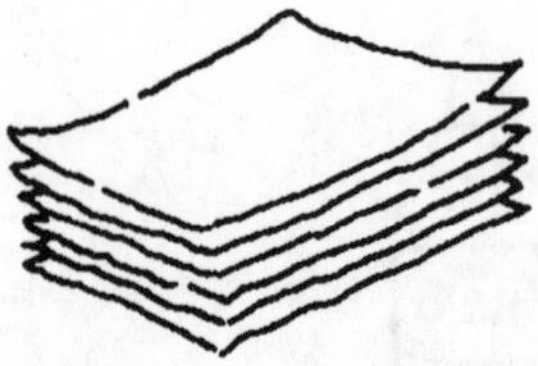

Score ______
(Top Score 5)

Teacher Read each word aloud. Tell students to look closely at each picture and draw a circle around the one that best relates to the word.

Vocabulary List

1. use
2. build
3. fit
4. tight
5. hammer
6. nail
7. brick
8. fix
9. glue
10. tools

4 Word Play

How Do You Make . . . ?

1. My uncle will ________ a doghouse for my dog.

   build glue

2. Please be sure that the door is closed ________.

   brick tight

3. Mom said that she would ________ us lunch.

   fix nail

4. ________ scissors to cut the paper.

   Use Tool

5. The mattress was too large to ________ through the door.

   hammer fit

Teacher Read each incomplete sentence aloud. Then read each word choice. Have students look closely at each word and draw a circle around the one that best completes the sentence.

Score ______
(Top Score 5)

"Jobs" Vocabulary

1 Word Meanings

Picture Clues

1. doctor

2. dentist

3. farmer

4. artist

5. cashier

A.

B.

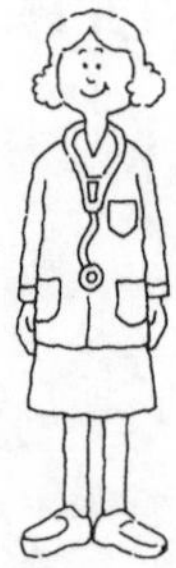

C.

D.

E.

Score ______
(Top Score 5)

Teacher Read each word aloud. Tell students to look closely at each picture. Have them draw a line from the word to the picture that it best matches.

Vocabulary List
1. work
2. carry
3. make
4. hold
5. doctor
6. nurse
7. dentist
8. farmer
9. artist
10. cashier

2 Reference Skills

The Suffix *-er*

1. farmer

A. 

2. dancer

B. 

3. reader

C. 

4. swimmer

D. 

5. runner

E. 

Teacher Read each word aloud. Tell students to look closely at the pictures. Have them draw a line from the word to the picture that it best matches.

Score ______
(Top Score 5)

3 Build New Vocabulary

Word Webs

1.

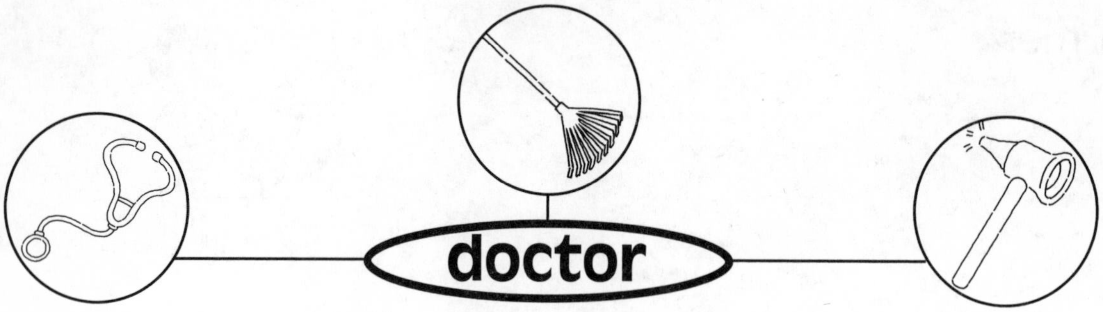
doctor

2.

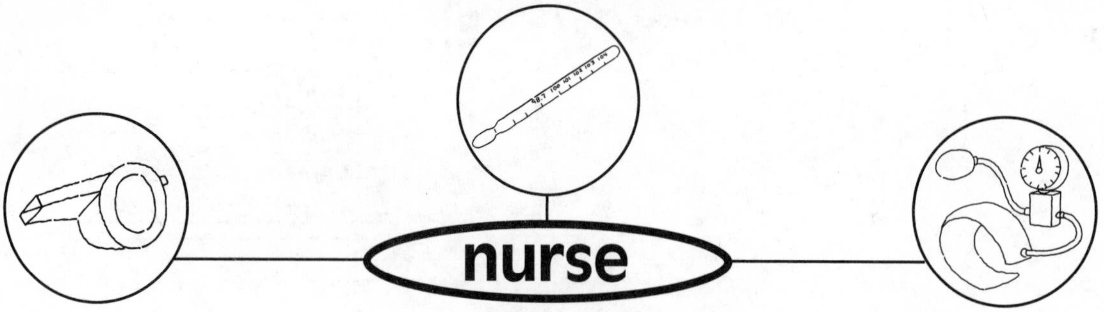
nurse

3.

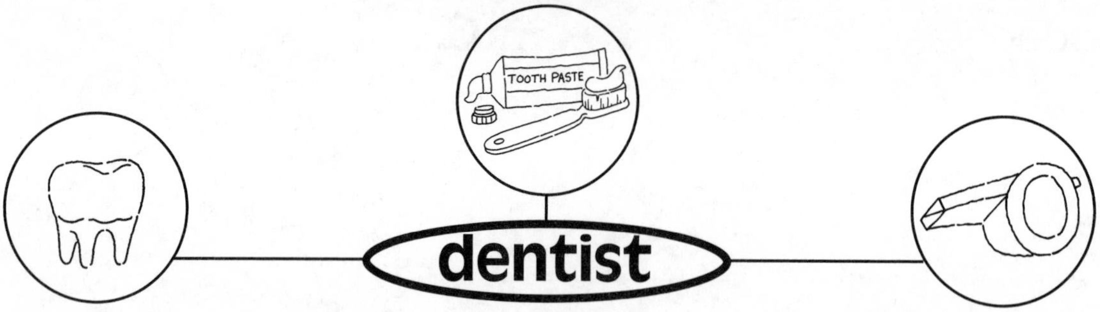
TOOTH PASTE
dentist

4.

artist

5.

cashier

Score _____
(Top Score 5)

Teacher For each word web, read the center vocabulary word aloud. Tell students to look closely at the three pictures in the smaller circles. Have them draw an X over the picture that is not associated with the vocabulary word.

Vocabulary List

1. work
2. carry
3. make
4. hold
5. doctor
6. nurse
7. dentist
8. farmer
9. artist
10. cashier

4 Word Play

When I Grow Up . . .

1. The ____ listened to my heartbeat.

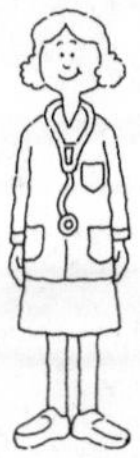 

2. The ____ counted all my teeth.

3. The ____ milked the cow.

4. The ____ took my temperature.

5. The ____ painted a picture.

Teacher Read each incomplete sentence aloud. Tell students to listen carefully to the sentence as they look at each picture. Have them draw a circle around the answer that best completes the sentence.

Score ____
(Top Score 5)

Vocabulary Review

1 Review Word Meanings

1. Texas is the second largest <u>state</u> in the United States.

 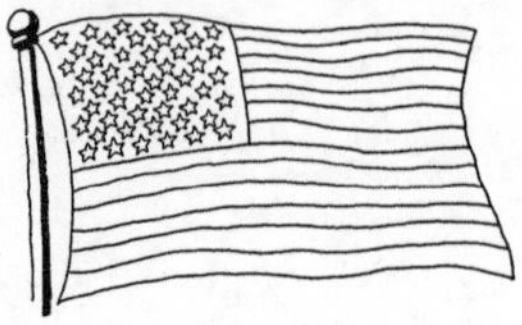 

2. Texas is the second largest state in the <u>United States</u>.

 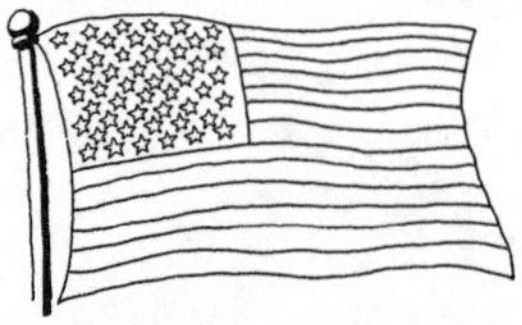 

3. My father talks about becoming a <u>doctor</u> or a nurse so he can help people who are sick.

4. He could also become a <u>dentist</u> who gives advice to people on how to care for their teeth.

5. He could also become a dentist who <u>gives</u> advice to people on how to care for their teeth.

Score ______
(Top Score 5)

Teacher Read the story on page 118 in the ***Teacher's Edition*** OR read each sentence above. Tell students to draw a circle around the picture that best matches each underlined word.

2 Review Word Meanings

1. My father thinks that he would like to be a farmer and raise cows and pigs.

ABC

2. He says that we could even raise goldfish and grasshoppers, if we wanted to.

3. He says that the whole family could work together to take care of the farm.

4. My father says that in the United States he could even become an artist.

5. He could use paints and paintbrushes to create beautiful pictures, or he could use special tools to make clay into pottery.

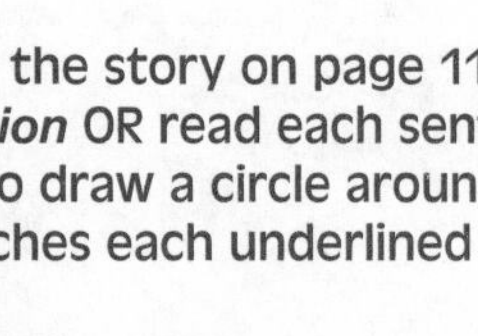

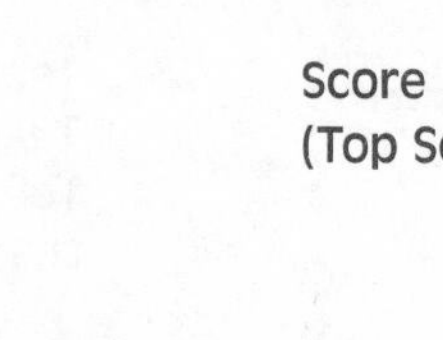

Teacher Read the story on page 119 in the ***Teacher's Edition*** OR read each sentence above. Tell students to draw a circle around the answer that best matches each underlined word.

Score _____
(Top Score 5)

3 Review Word Meanings

1. My father imagines being a cashier at my favorite store.

2. He considers becoming a construction worker who would carry a hammer and nails with him.

 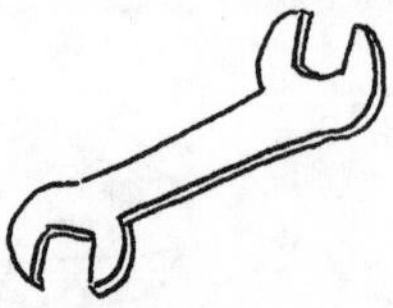 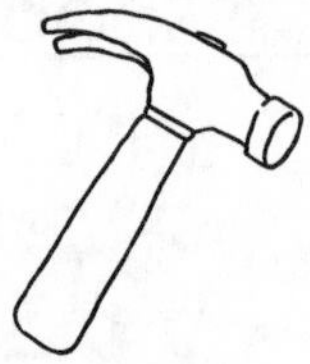

3. He says that he could build new houses with brick or fix old houses with glue, plaster, and paint.

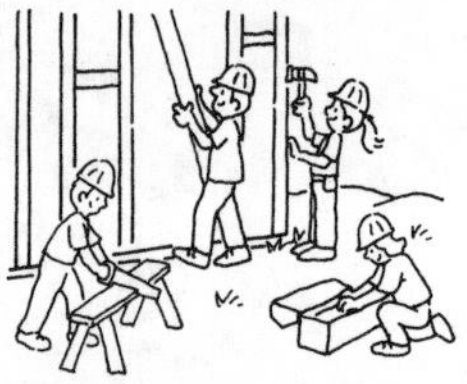  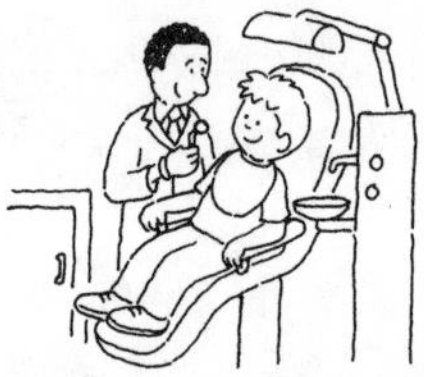

4. He says that he could build new houses with brick or fix old houses with glue, plaster, and paint.

  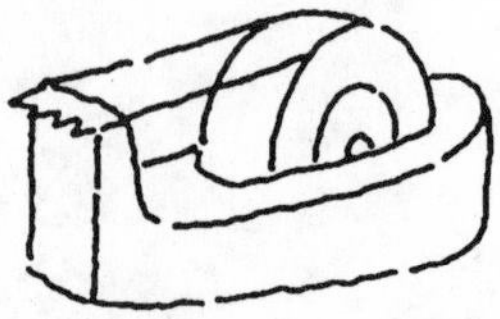

5. He would make sure that each house had a birdhouse for the backyard and a flag for the front porch.

Score ______
(Top Score 5)

Teacher Read the story on page 120 in the ***Teacher's Edition*** OR read each sentence above. Tell students to draw a circle around the answer that best matches each underlined word.

4 Review Word Meanings

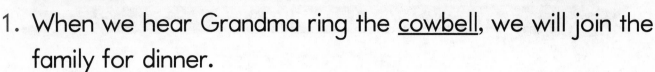

1. When we hear Grandma ring the cowbell, we will join the family for dinner.

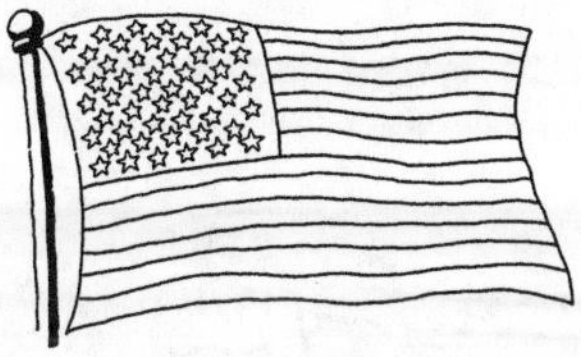  

2. Grandpa raises bees, and tonight he has brought honey from his beehive.

  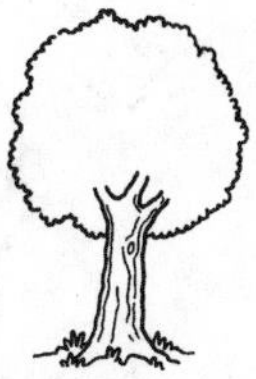

3. The catfish smells wonderful, and we can hardly wait to eat.

4. Suddenly, the bulldog starts barking wildly!

5. He has found another anthill in the yard.

  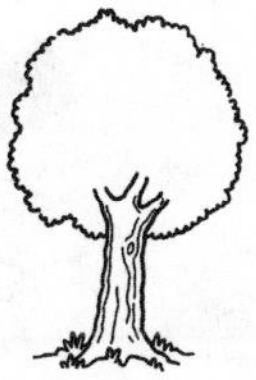

Teacher Read the story on page 121 in the ***Teacher's Edition*** OR read each sentence above. Tell students to draw a circle around the answer that best matches each underlined word.

Score ______
(Top Score 5)

"By the Sea" Vocabulary

1 Word Meanings

By Land and By Sea

1. boat

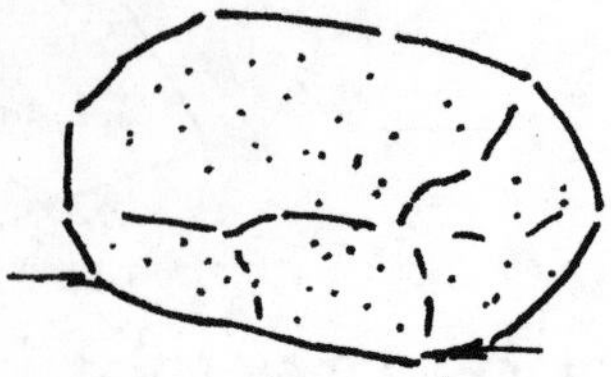 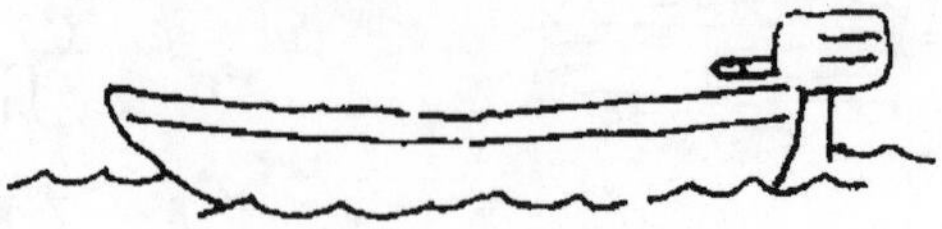

2. shell

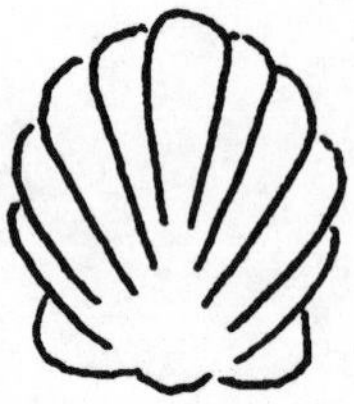 

3. rock

 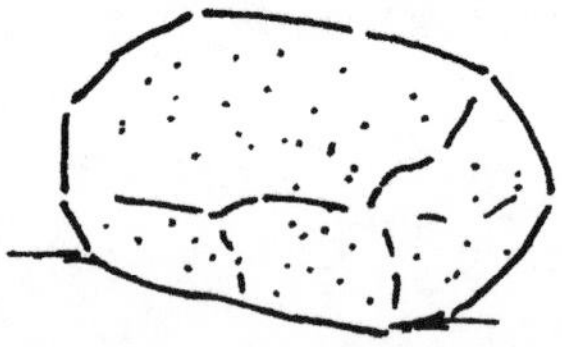

4. beach

5. sail

 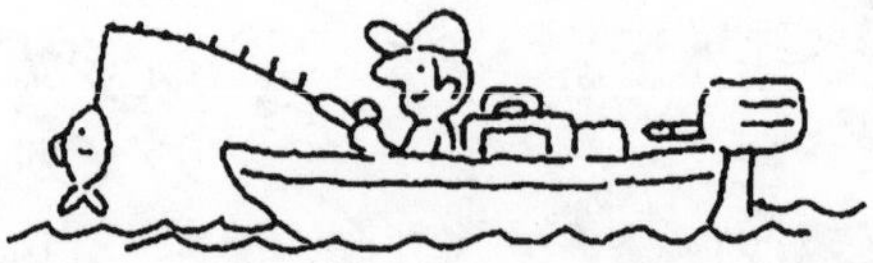

Score ______
(Top Score 5)

Teacher Read each word aloud. Tell students to look closely at each picture. Have them draw a circle around the picture that best matches the word.

Vocabulary List		
1. aboard	3. beach	7. shell
2. sail	4. bay	8. rock
	5. boat	9. shore
	6. deep	10. ship

2 Reference Skills

Alphabetical Order

A B C D E F G H I J K L M N
O P Q R S T U V W X Y Z
a b c d e f g h i j k l m n o
p q r s t u v w x y z

_____ deep

_____ bay

_____ rock

_____ beach

_____ aboard

Teacher Read each word aloud. Tell students to begin with the number 1 and number each word as it would appear in alphabetical order. Have them refer to the alphabet chart for assistance.

Score _____
(Top Score 5)

3 Build New Vocabulary

Sail Away!

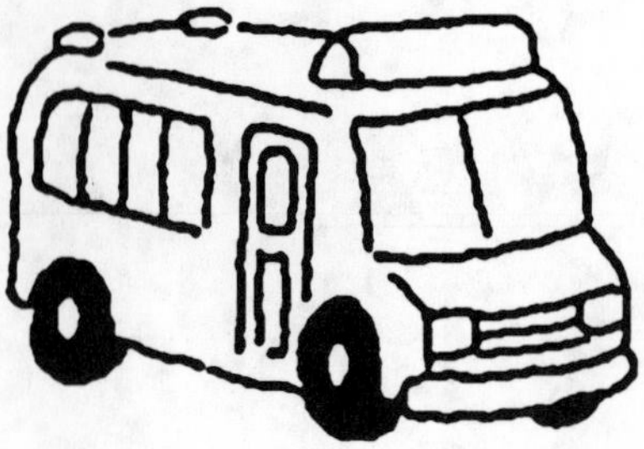
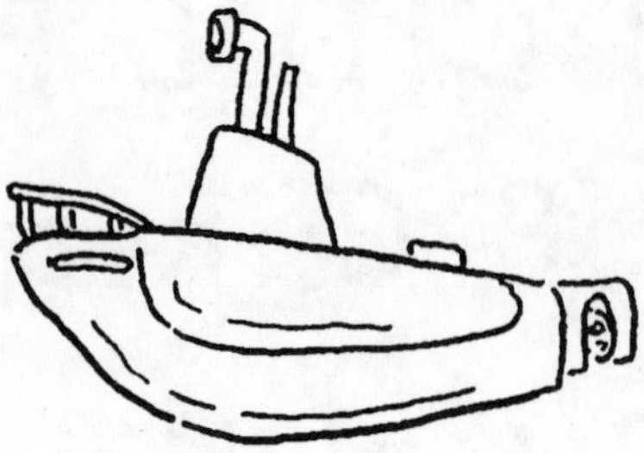
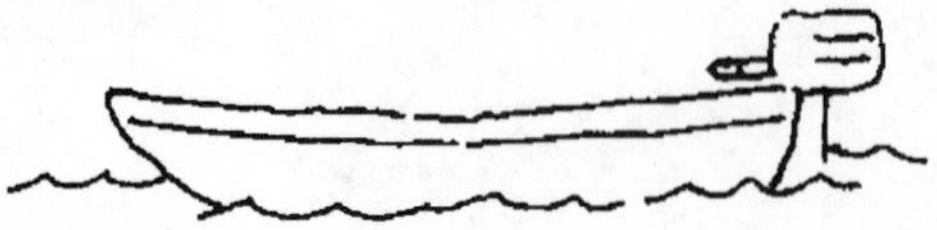

Score ______
(Top Score 3)

Teacher Tell students to look closely at each picture. Have them draw an X over the images that do NOT travel through water.

Vocabulary List
1. aboard
2. sail
3. beach
4. bay
5. boat
6. deep
7. shell
8. rock
9. shore
10. ship

4 Word Play

The Little Ship That Could

1. The captain of the ____ waved to us.

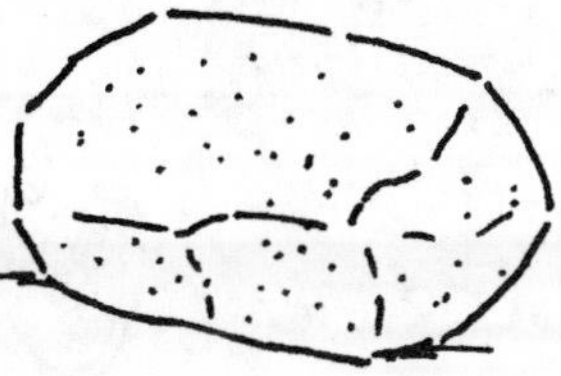

2. We all went aboard the ____.

3. She held the ____ to her ear and listened.

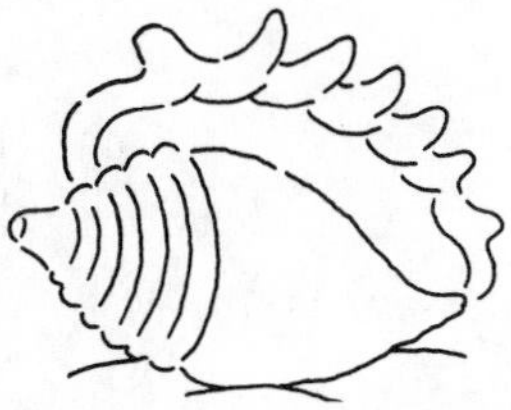

4. They built a sand castle on the ____.

5. The large turtle was lying on the ____.

Teacher Read each incomplete sentence aloud. Tell students to listen carefully to each sentence while looking at the pictures below it. Have them draw a circle around the picture that best completes the sentence.

Score ____
(Top Score 5)

"Sound Alike" Vocabulary

1 Word Meanings

Sound Alike, Look Different

1. ant

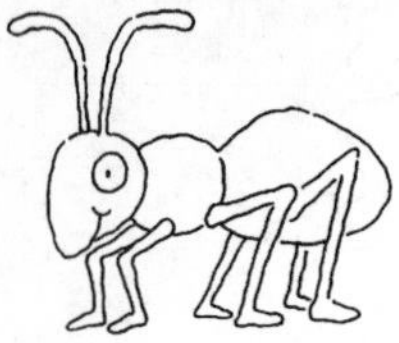

2. bear

3. flower

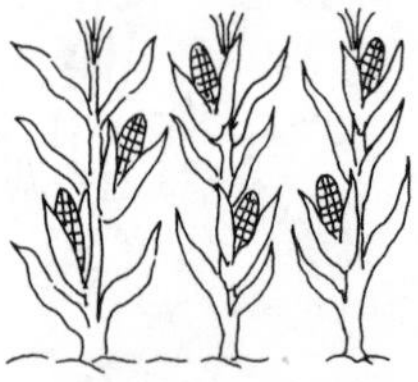

4. sun

5. hare

Score ______
(Top Score 5)

Teacher Read each word aloud. Tell students to look closely at each picture. Have them draw a circle around the picture that best matches the word.

Vocabulary List		
1. bear	3. hair	7. flower
2. bare	4. hare	8. flour
	5. son	9. aunt
	6. sun	10. ant

2 Reference Skills

Which Is It?

1. Mrs. Smith is also my aunt.

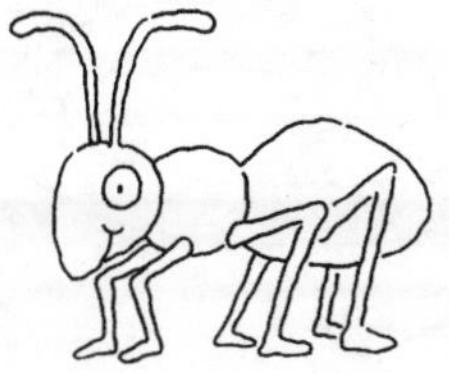

2. The cupboard was bare.

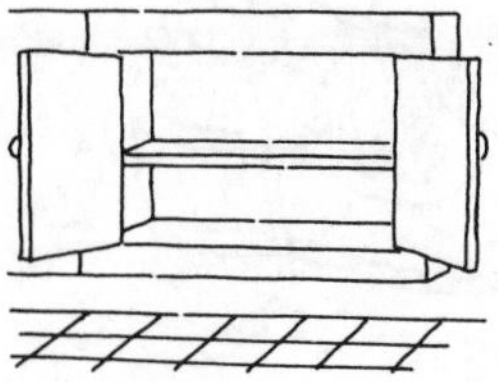

3. Bakers use flour to make bread.

XX

4. The father wrote a letter to his son.

5. The hare hopped through the field.

Teacher Read each sentence aloud. Tell students to listen carefully and look closely at each picture below. Have them draw a circle around the picture that matches the underlined word in each sentence.

Score _____
(Top Score 5)

3 Build New Vocabulary

Homophones: Words That Sound Alike

1. Our dog has eight puppies.

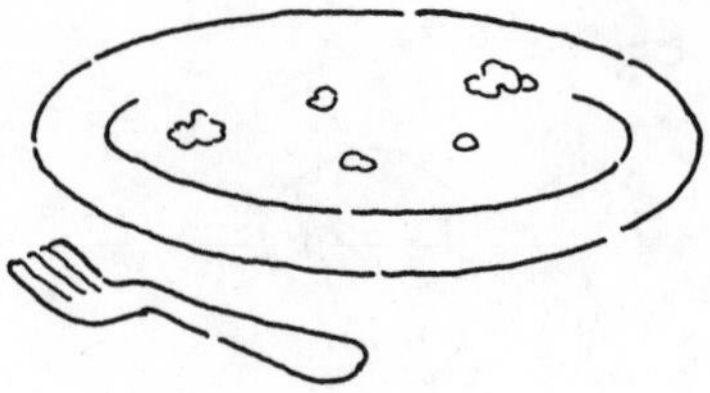

2. The pear was juicy and sweet.

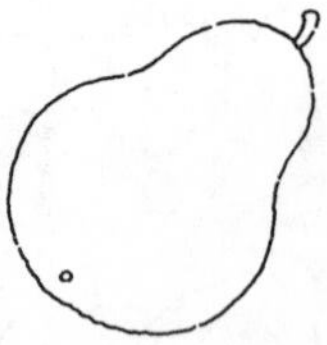

3. We are learning to write our names.

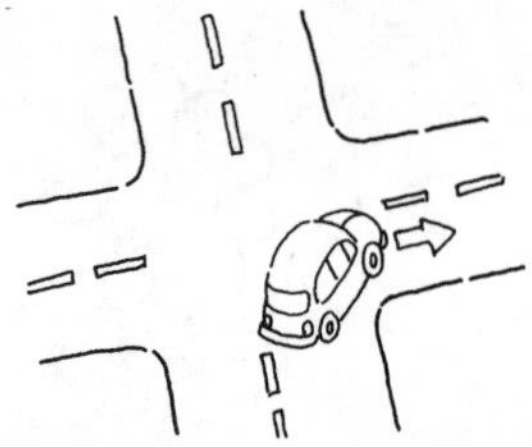

4. The bee landed on my toe.

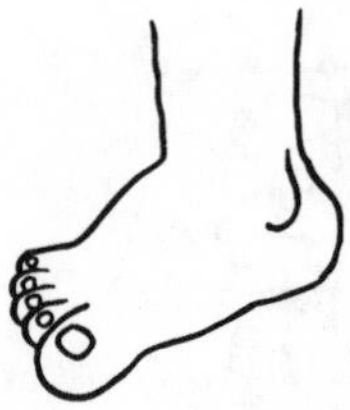

5. You put golf balls on a tee.

Score ______
(Top Score 5)

Teacher Read each sentence aloud. Repeat the underlined word in each. Have students draw a circle around the picture that best matches the underlined word.

Vocabulary List
1. bear
2. bare
3. hair
4. hare
5. son
6. sun
7. flower
8. flour
9. aunt
10. ant

4 Word Play

Silly Sentences

1. hare

A. 

2. hair

B. 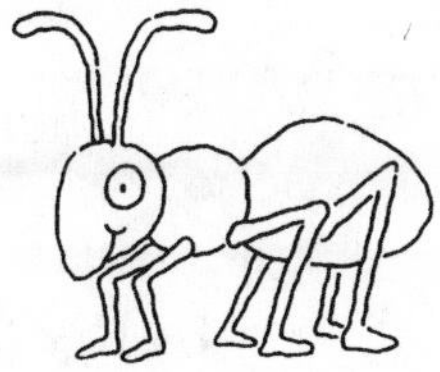

3. ant

C. 

4. aunt

D. 

5. bare

E. 

6. bear

F. 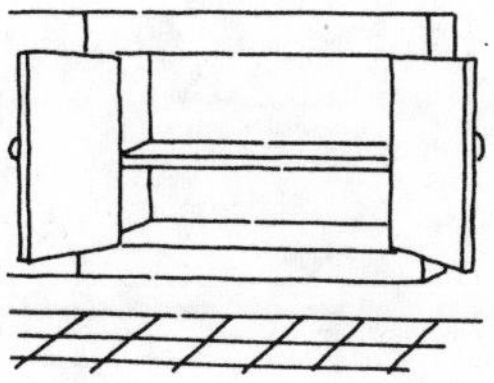

Teacher Read each word aloud. Tell students to look closely at each picture in the right-hand column. Have them draw a line from the word on the left to the picture on the right that matches.

Score ______
(Top Score 6)

Vocabulary for Nature

1 Word Meanings

Examples/Nonexamples

1. leaf

A. 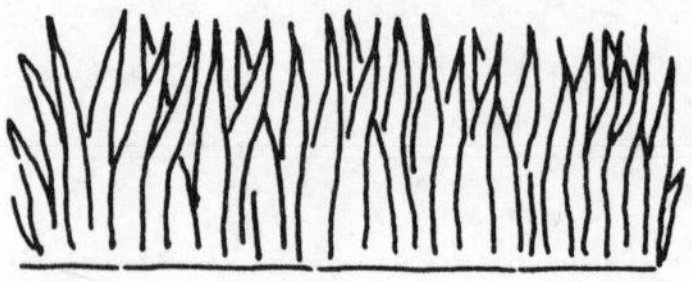

2. grass

B. 

3. vegetable

C. 

4. nut

D. 

5. garden

E. 

Score _____
(Top Score 5)

Teacher Read each word aloud. Have students draw a line from the word on the left to the picture on the right that it best matches.

Vocabulary List		
1. fruit	3. grass	7. nut
2. garden	4. Earth	8. vegetable
	5. leaf	9. pond
	6. tree	10. insect

2 Reference Skills

Picture Dictionary

1. fruit

2. Earth

3. tree

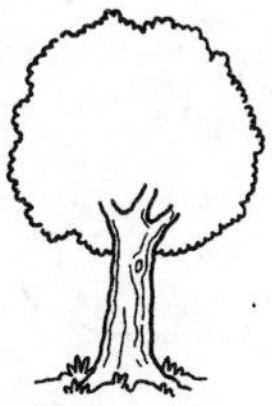

4. pond

5. insect

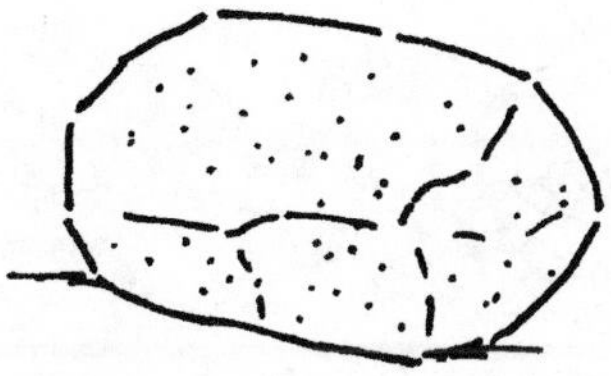

Teacher Read each word aloud. Tell students to look closely at the pictures below each word. Have them draw a circle around the picture that matches the word.

Score ______
(Top Score 5)

3 Build New Vocabulary

Different Kinds of Things

1. Mother says ____ is a healthy snack.

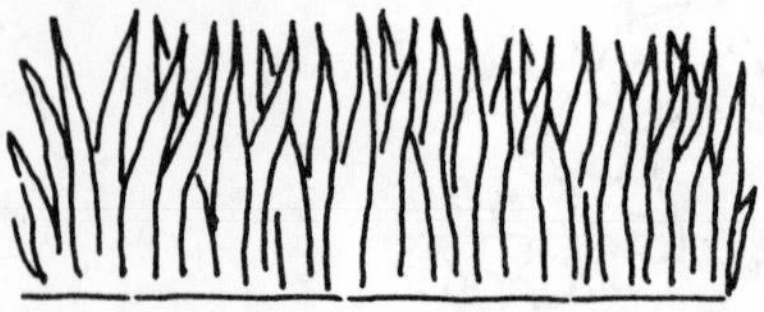

2. She picked apples off of the ____.

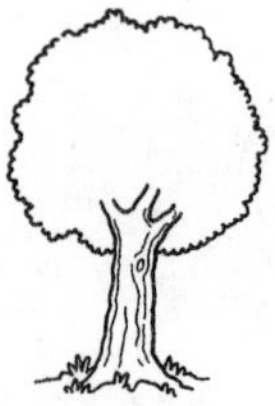

3. We had to rake up all the ____.

4. Mrs. Jones grows tomatoes in her ____.

5. Uncle Bill mows our ____ with a lawn mower.

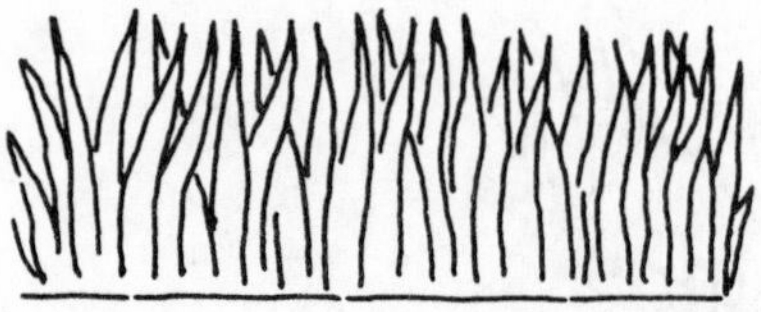

Score ____
(Top Score 5)

Teacher Read each incomplete sentence aloud. Have students draw a circle around the picture that best completes the sentence.

Vocabulary List		
1. fruit	3. grass	7. nut
2. garden	4. Earth	8. vegetable
	5. leaf	9. pond
	6. tree	10. insect

4 Word Play

Favorite Nature Place

1. nut

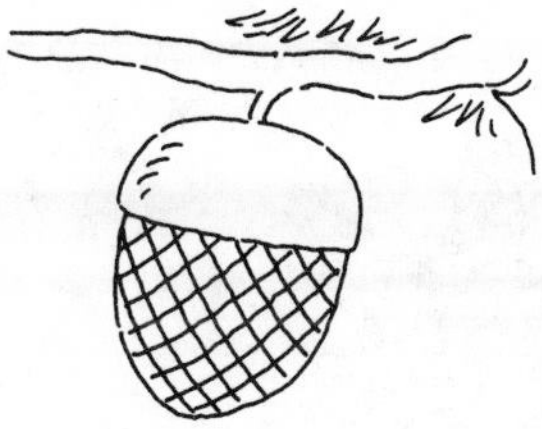

2. pond

3. insect

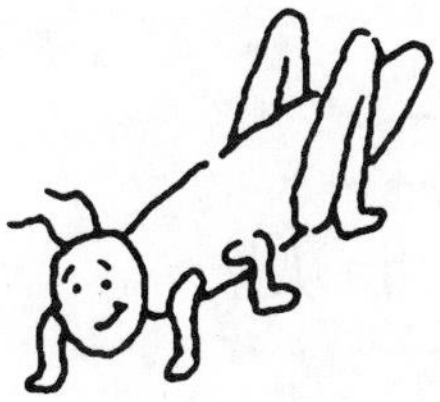

4. fruit

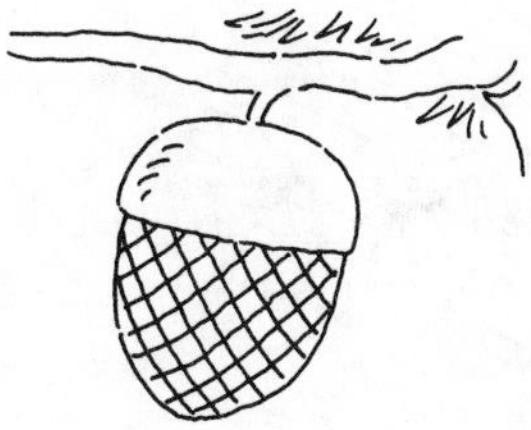

5. tree

Teacher Read each word aloud. Tell students to look closely at the pictures below each word. Have them draw an X over the picture that does NOT match the word.

Score ______
(Top Score 5)

"Action Words" Vocabulary

1 Word Meanings

Show the Action

1. ride

2. lift

 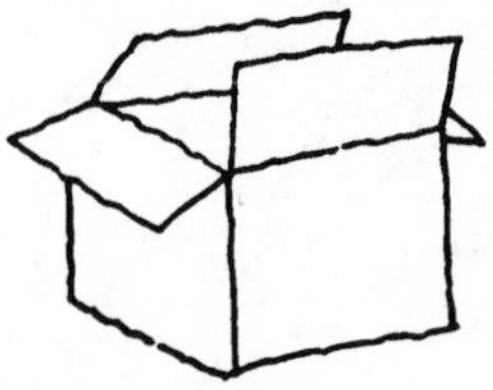

3. fast

4. slow

5. walk

Score _____
(Top Score 5)

Teacher Read each word aloud. Tell students to look closely at each picture. Have them draw a circle around the picture that best matches the vocabulary word.

Vocabulary List
1. bring
2. cut
3. fast
4. find
5. lift
6. pick
7. ride
8. slow
9. take
10. walk

2 Reference Skills

Action Words vs. Nonaction Words

1. bring

THE
UGLY
DUCKLING

ABC

2. cut

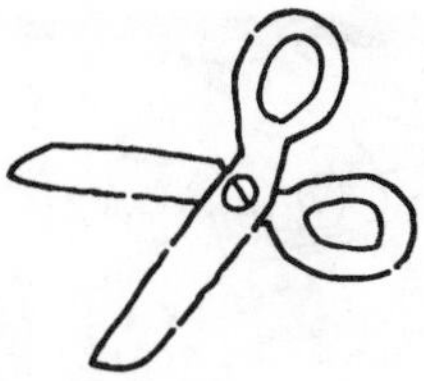

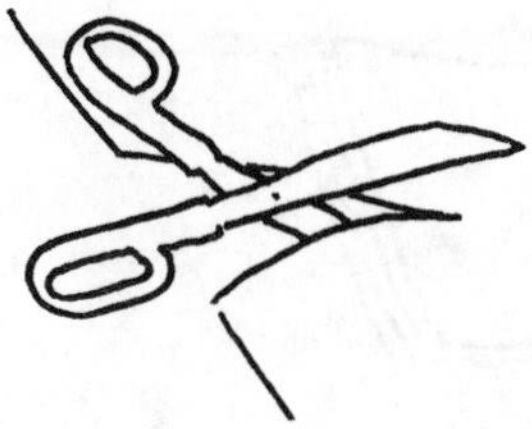

3. find

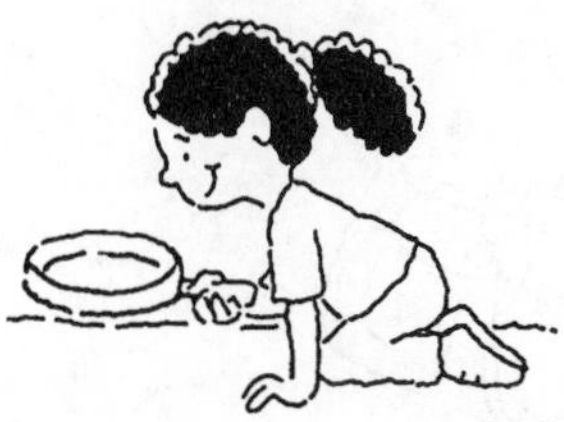

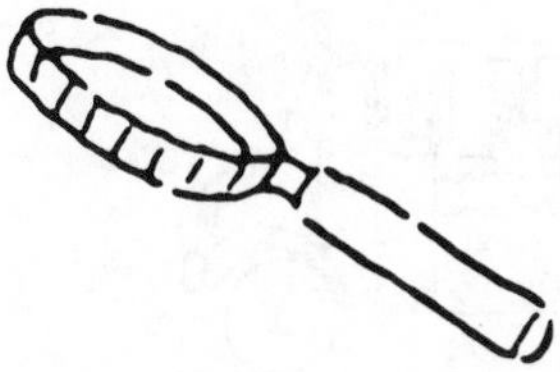

4. pick

5. ride

Teacher Read each word aloud. Tell students to look closely at each picture. Have them draw an X over the picture that is NOT an action.

Score ______
(Top Score 5)

3 Build New Vocabulary

More Action Words

1. I can walk fast.

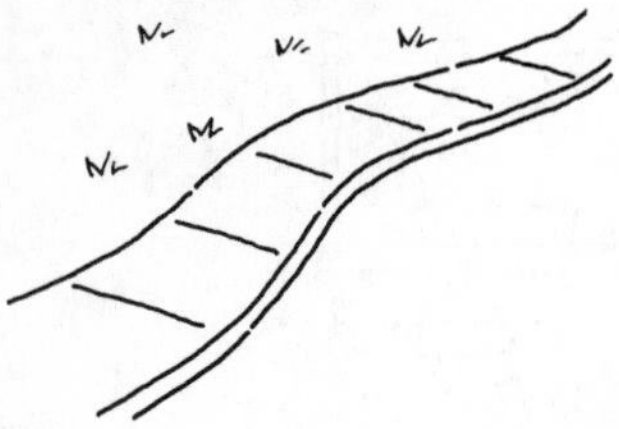

2. Please cut the paper.

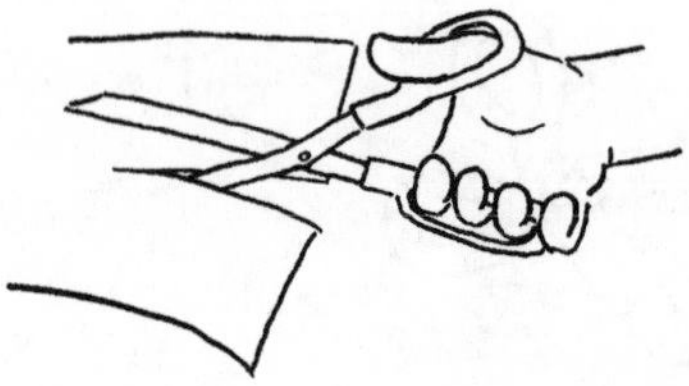

3. Did you ride the bus?

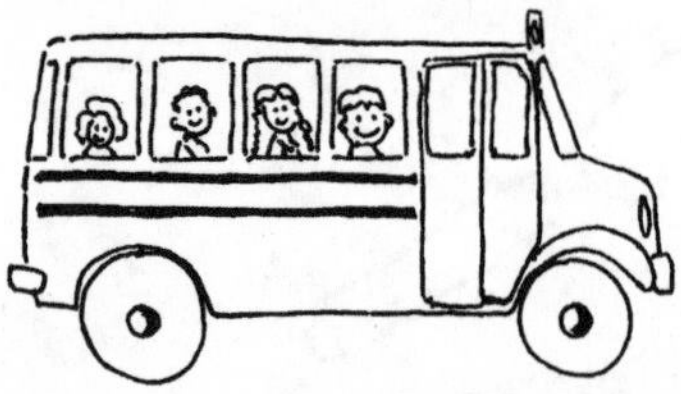

4. He can run a mile.

5. She likes to dance.

Score _____
(Top Score 5)

Teacher Read each sentence aloud. Repeat the underlined action word. Have students draw a circle around the picture that best matches the action word.

Vocabulary List
1. bring
2. cut
3. fast
4. find
5. lift
6. pick
7. ride
8. slow
9. take
10. walk

4 Word Play

Action Charades

1. lift

2. pick

3. walk

4. cut

5. bring

A.

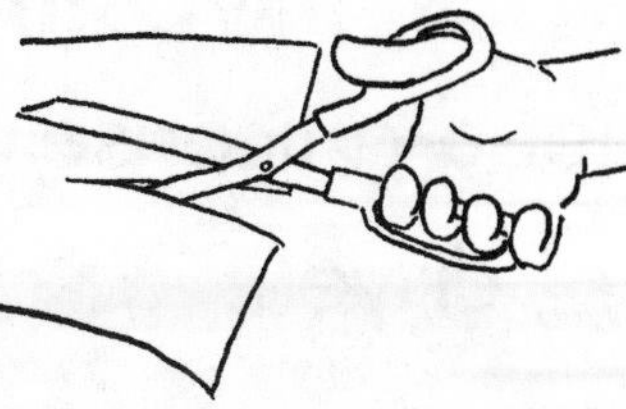

B.

C.

ABC

D.

E.

Teacher Read each word aloud. Have students draw a line from the word on the left to the picture on the right that it best matches.

Score ______
(Top Score 5)

Vocabulary for Cars

1 Word Meanings

Complete the Sentence

1. You need a license to ____ a car.

   drive curb hood

2. The ____ covers the back part of a car.

   trunk hood windshield

3. A ____ shines light onto the road when it is dark.

   sign pedal headlight

4. The edge of a sidewalk is called a ____.

   license curb hood

5. Press the ____ with your foot to make the car go.

   pedal trunk sign

Score ____
(Top Score 5)

Teacher Read each sentence and each possible answer aloud. Have students circle the word that best completes each sentence.

Vocabulary List
1. sidewalk
2. curb
3. sign
4. windshield
5. trunk
6. hood
7. headlight
8. pedal
9. license
10. drive

2 Reference Skills

Using a Dictionary

A	B	C	D	E	F	G	H	I	J	K	L	M	N
O	P	Q	R	S	T	U	V	W	X	Y	Z		
a	b	c	d	e	f	g	h	i	j	k	l	m	n	o
p	q	r	s	t	u	v	w	x	y	z			

1. hood headlight windshield

2. drive sidewalk sign

3. curb drive trunk

4. pedal windshield license

5. headlight sign trunk

Teacher Read each set of words aloud. Point out the underlined letter in each word. Have students cross out the word that would NOT be found in the same part of the dictionary as the other two words.

Score ____
(Top Score 5)

3 Build New Vocabulary

More Than One Meaning

1. A hood keeps your head warm.

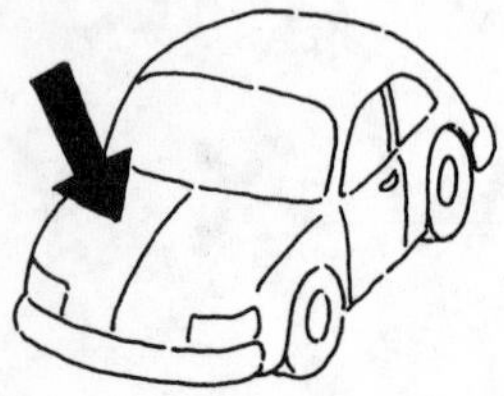
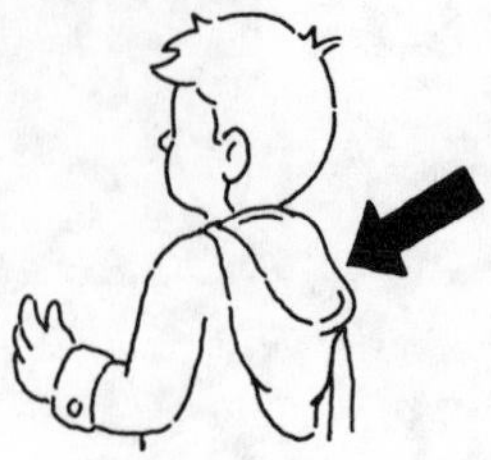

2. The trunk of that tree is huge!

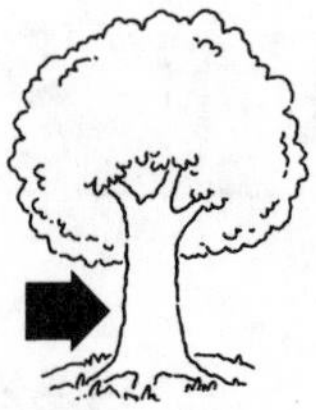

3. We carry groceries in the trunk of our car.

4. Open the hood to check the oil.

5. I found a trunk full of toys in the basement.

Score ______
(Top Score 5)

Teacher Read each sentence aloud. Have students draw a circle around the picture that matches the meaning of the underlined word in that sentence.

Vocabulary List
1. sidewalk
2. curb
3. sign
4. windshield
5. trunk
6. hood
7. headlight
8. pedal
9. license
10. drive

4 Word Play

Same Letter Sounds

1. Watch the worms wiggling on the ____.

sidewalk   windshield   curb

2. Did Daphne ____ Diego down to Detroit for dinner?

drive   headlight   pedal

3. Sid was sore after sliding into the ____ on his skateboard.

hood   curb   sign

4. Let's look at Linus's ____ in the light.

license   headlight   windshield

5. Heavy hail from the hurricane hit his ____.

trunk   hood   pedal

Teacher Read each sentence and each possible answer aloud. Have students circle the word that has the same beginning sound as most of the other words in the sentence.

Score ____
(Top Score 5)

Vocabulary Review

1 Review Word Meanings

1. My brother Ben and I went to visit our aunt.

2. She had a scavenger hunt ready for us and told us to follow the sign at each stopping point.

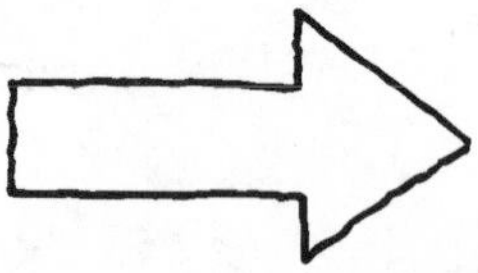

3. Aunt Marie said some of the items could be found on the beach and some could be found in the woods.

4. While we were on our scavenger hunt, Aunt Marie said she had to get her hair cut.

5. She said she would be home before the sun went down.

Score ______
(Top Score 5)

Teacher Read aloud the story on page 142 in the ***Teacher's Edition*** OR read the sentences above for each number. Tell students to draw a circle around the picture that best matches the underlined vocabulary word.

2 Review Word Meanings

1. Ben and I walked down the path behind Aunt Marie's house to the beach.

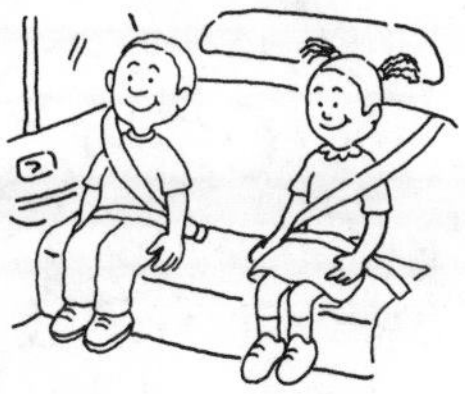  

2. The first thing we had to find was a shell.

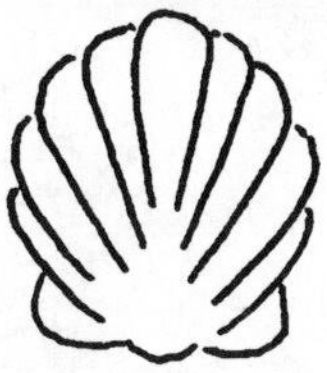  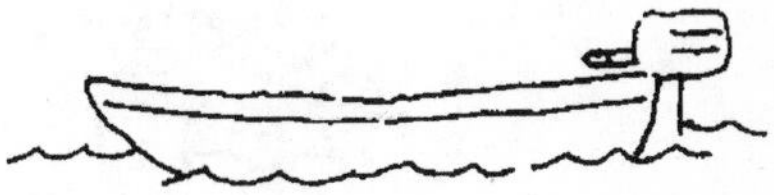

3. We walked along the shore looking for the perfect shell.

4. The second item on our list was a rock.

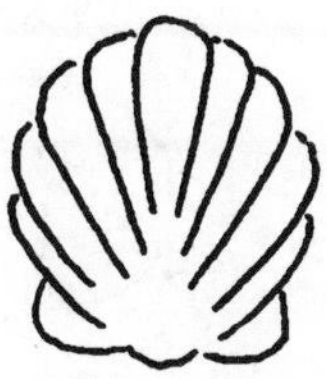 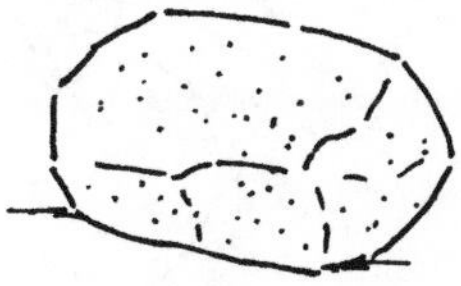 

5. The small boat that Aunt Marie owned was the perfect way to get to the woods.

Teacher Read aloud the story on page 143 in the *Teacher's Edition* OR read the sentences above for each number. Tell students to draw a circle around the picture that best matches the underlined vocabulary word.

Score _____
(Top Score 5)

3 Review Word Meanings

1. We opened the bag and found two pieces of fruit—an apple and a pear.

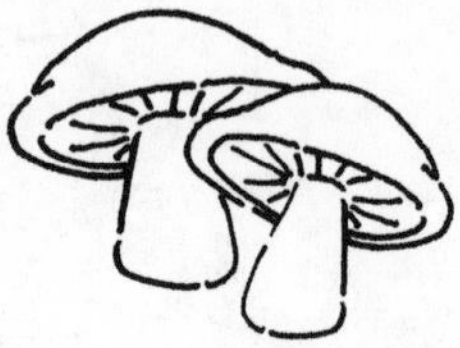

2. Ben and I pretended our boat was a large ship sailing across the deep ocean.

3. The woods were filled with tall trees.

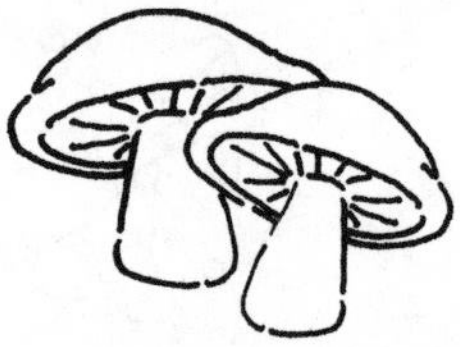

4. The next item on our list was a leaf.

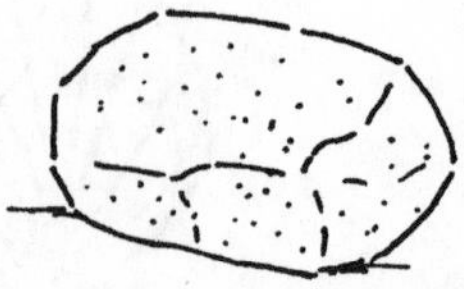

5. We needed a type of nut called an acorn to finish our scavenger hunt.

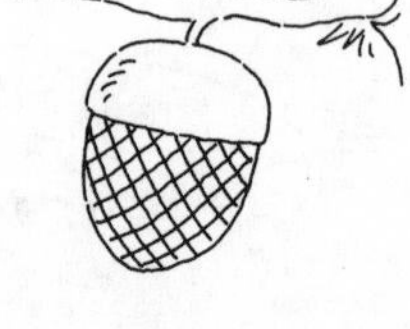
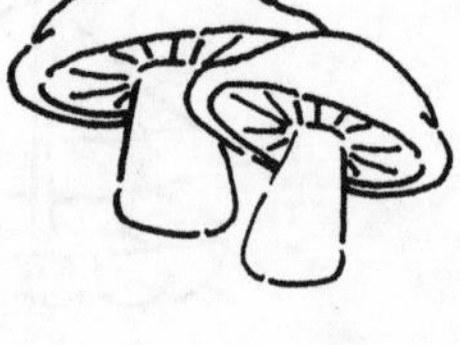

Score ______
(Top Score 5)

Teacher Read aloud the story on page 144 in the ***Teacher's Edition*** OR read the sentences above for each number. Tell students to draw a circle around the picture that best matches the underlined vocabulary word.

4 Review Word Meanings

1. A brown hare came out of the grass and hopped right by us.

2. We sure were glad that the hare was not a bear!

3. There was an ant trying to carry an acorn all by itself.

4. When we got back to her house, she was working in her garden.

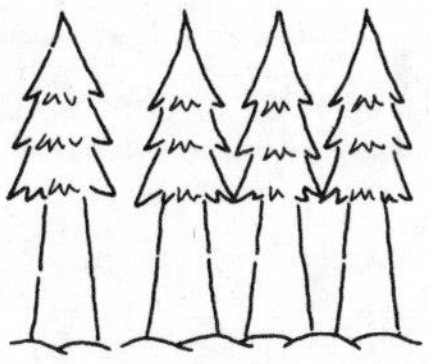  

5. She rewarded us with a special flower from her garden.

  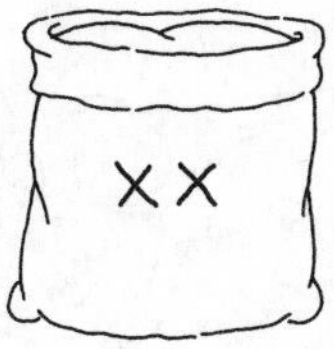
XX

Teacher Read aloud the story on page 145 in the ***Teacher's Edition*** OR read the sentences above for each number. Tell students to draw a circle around the picture that best matches the underlined vocabulary word.

Score ______
(Top Score 5)

Cumulative Review

1 Review Word Meanings

Definitions

1. 

off over under

2. 

windmill storm breeze

3. 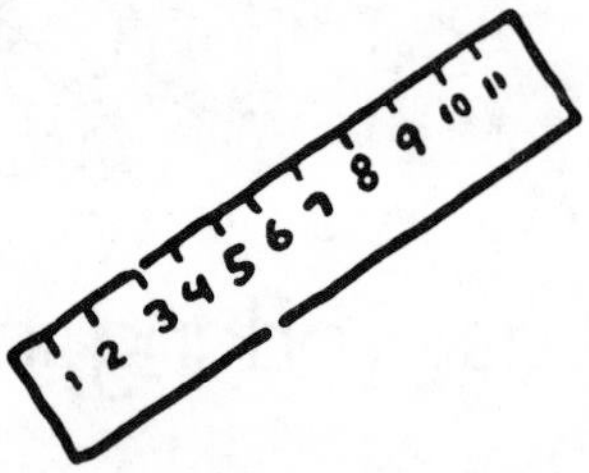
1 2 3 4 5 6 7 8 9 10 11

ruler pencil desk

4. 

once before between

5. 

race reach goal

Score ______
(Top Score 5)

Teacher Tell students to look carefully at each picture as you read each word choice aloud. Have them circle the word that represents the picture.

2 Review Word Meanings

Synonyms

1.

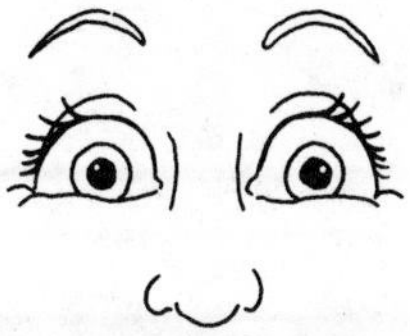

look run see

2.

sick afraid scare

3.

quick fast furry

4.

happy cry glad

5.

slide hop jump

Teacher Tell students to look carefully at each picture as you read each word choice aloud. Have them cross out the word that does NOT represent the picture.

Score _____
(Top Score 5)

3 Review Word Meanings

Sentence Completion

1. You can hear a bee ____.

buzz

meow

2. Mom put the packages into the ____.

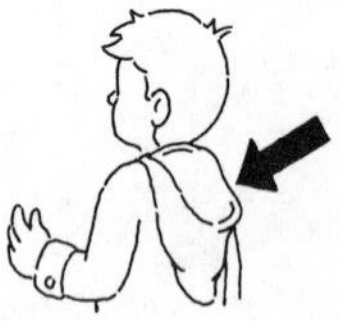
hood

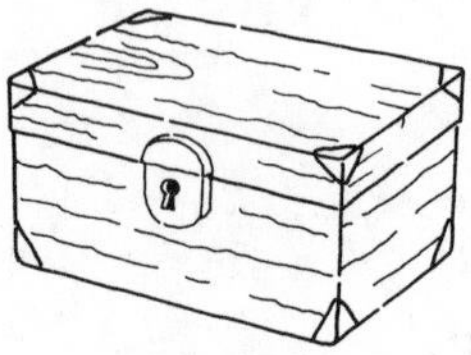
trunk

3. We ride our sleds in the ____.

winter

autumn

4. You have to ____ the lawn mower to cut the grass.

laugh

push

5. Please mail my letters at the ____.

POST OFFICE
MAIL
post office

STATION NO. 12
firehouse

Score ____
(Top Score 5)

Teacher Tell students to listen carefully as you read each sentence aloud. Have them circle the word-picture combination that best completes the sentence.

Words and Themes

1.  backyard — Touch

2.  shell — Playground

3. 
MAY
month — By the Sea

4.  swing — Home

5.  smooth — Red, White, and Blue

6.  American — Calendar

Teacher Read each word and theme aloud. Tell students to draw a line from the word on the left to the correct theme on the right. Have them complete this exercise without looking back at the Vocabulary Lists in each lesson.

Score ______
(Top Score 6)

Word Webs

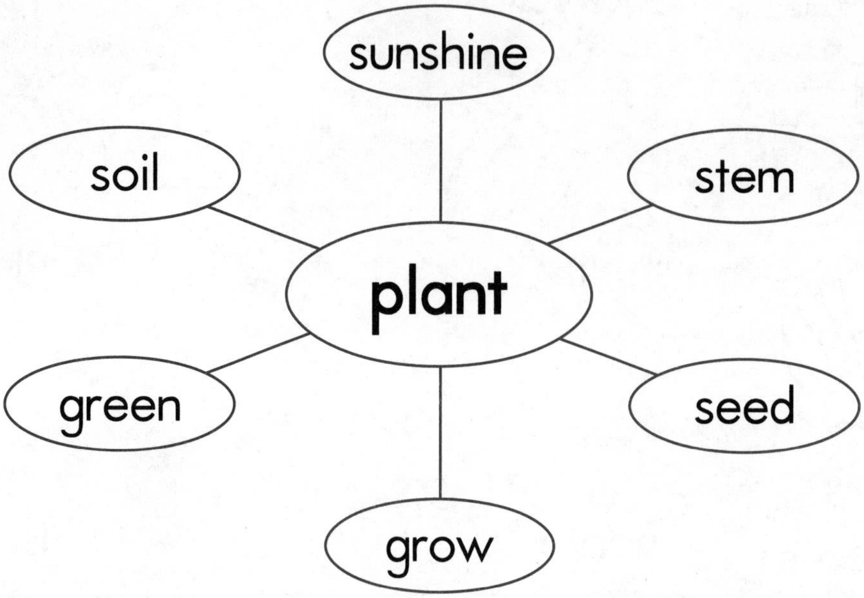
sunshine
soil
stem
plant
green
seed
grow

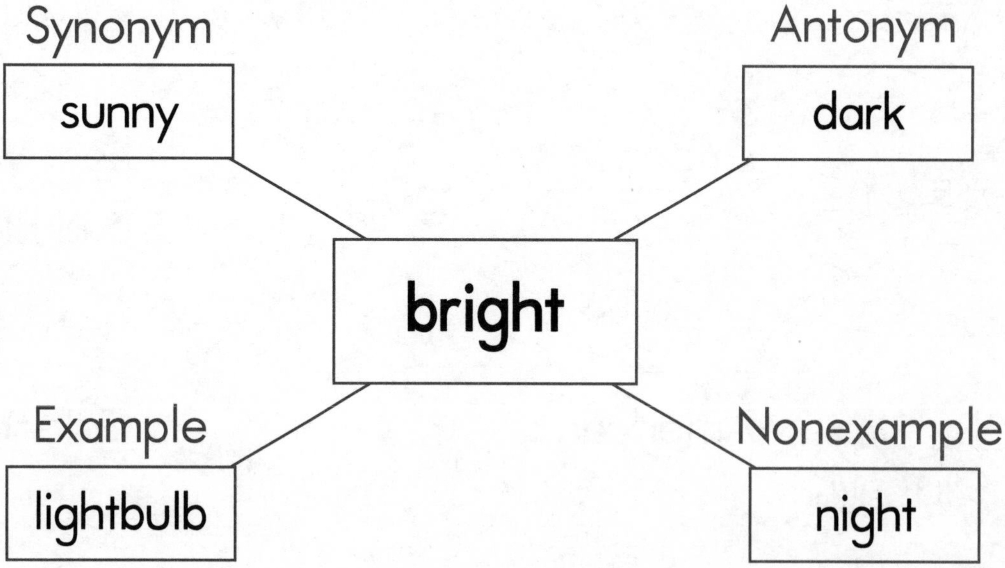
Synonym
sunny
Antonym
dark
bright
Example
lightbulb
Nonexample
night

Categorization

Words That Begin With "b"

bang
bank
book
bulletin board
blustery

BOOK

Animals

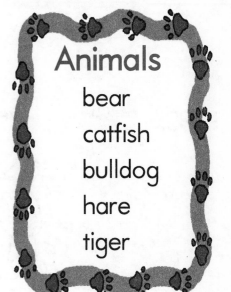

bear
catfish
bulldog
hare
tiger

Color Words

purple
yellow
green
red
blue

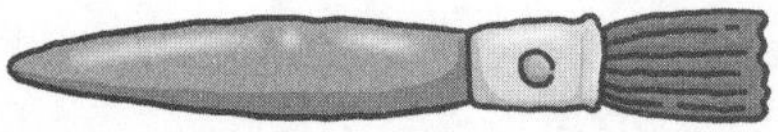

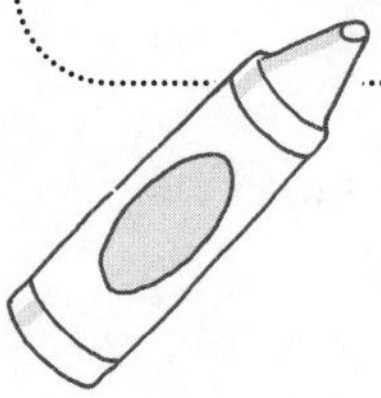

Winter Words

snow
ice
cold
sled
scarf
mittens

Linear Graphs

cold → cool → warm → hot

soggy → wet → damp → dry

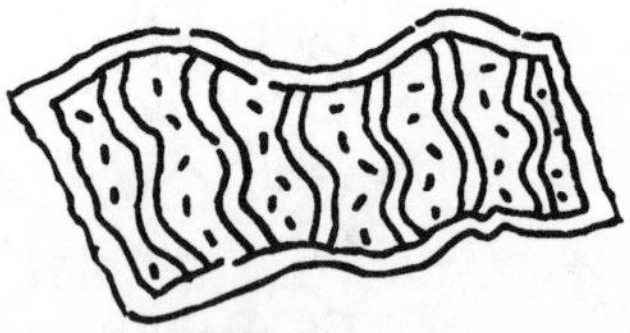

run → jog → walk → crawl

FINISH LINE

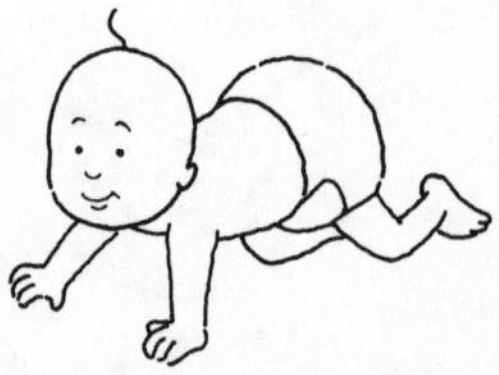

Context Clues

A **context clue** is a clue to the meaning of a word.

New Word

The ladybug is tiny.

Context Clue

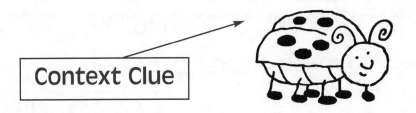

Tiny means "very small."

New Word

Dinosaur bones are ancient, or very old.

Context Clue

MUSEUM

Ancient means "very old."

Context Clues

You can use context clues when you read.

New Word

Context Clue

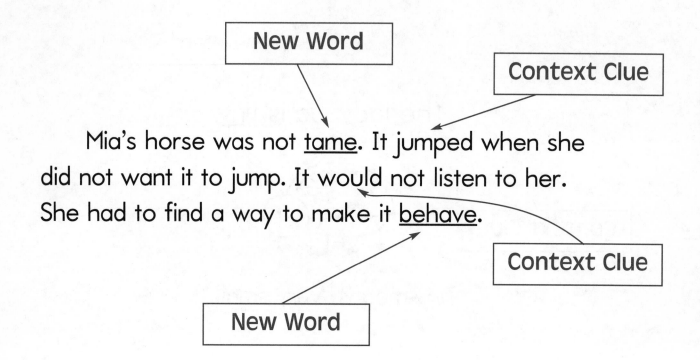

Mia's horse was not tame. It jumped when she did not want it to jump. It would not listen to her. She had to find a way to make it behave.

Context Clue

New Word

Tame means "gentle."

Behave means "to act properly."

Word Relationships

Antonyms have opposite meanings.

Antonyms

hot/cold	old/young
high/low	above/below
big/little	push/pull
tall/short	close/open

Synonyms have the same or about the same meanings.

Synonyms

begin/start	small/tiny
happy/glad	large/big
close/shut	fast/quick
old/ancient	yell/shout

Word Relationships

Word Families

The *at* Word Family

at	mat
cat	flat
hat	sat
bat	that

The *ay* Word Family

say	gray
may	clay
play	day
tray	ray

Homophones

I/eye	no/know	ate/eight
right/write	see/sea	ant/aunt

The ship sailed on the **sea.**

I **see** the storm coming.

Homographs

bat: a flying animal bat: a club for hitting a baseball	bark: the sound a dog makes bark: the covering of a tree

This old baseball **bat** is made of wood.

Bats fly at night.

SRA

Building Vocabulary Skills
Level K
Home Connection

To Reinforce Vocabulary Skills at Home

Tools and Reference

Table of Contents

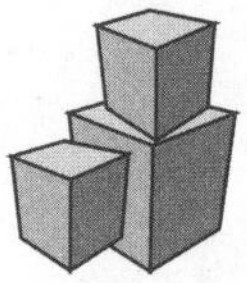

Words in Another Country .... T&R2
Prefixes and Suffixes .... T&R3
Base Words .... T&R4
Dolch Words .... T&R5
Fun With Words .... T&R6
Dictionary Skills .... T&R7
Nouns, Verbs, and Adjectives .... T&R9

Glossary .... T&R10

Word Bank .... T&R29

www.sra4kids.com

Send all inquiries to:
SRA/McGraw-Hill
8787 Orion Place
Columbus, OH 43240-4027

Printed in the United States of America.

R00004408

2 3 4 5 6 7 8 9 QPD 07 06 05 04 03

SRA

Columbus, OH • Chicago, IL • Redmond, WA

The McGraw·Hill Companies

Words in Another Country

Note to Home Use this page as a fun reference for pointing out the different words used for common objects in the United States and Great Britain. This will help your student begin to understand the cultural nature of words. You may wish to show your student where Great Britain is located on a map or globe.

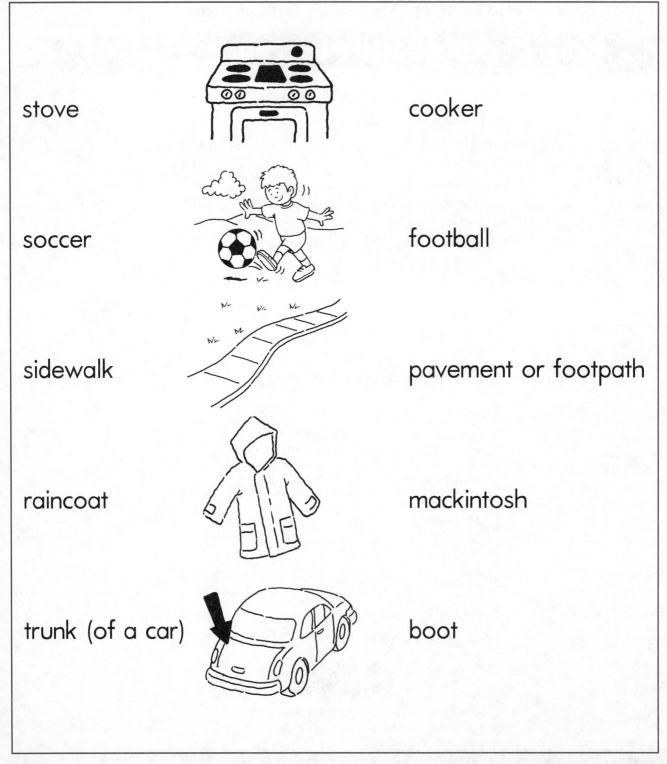

American Words		British Words
stove		cooker
soccer		football
sidewalk	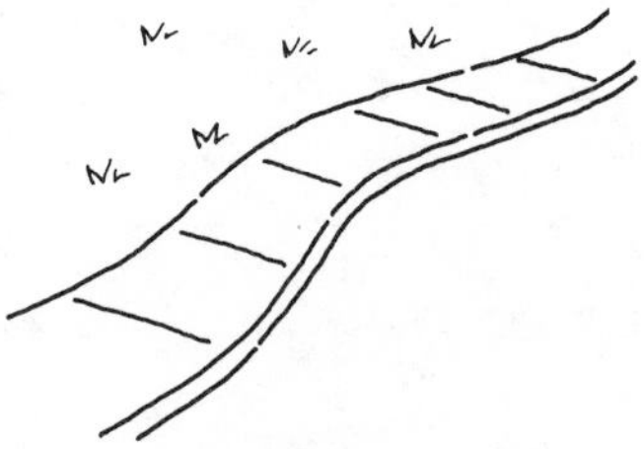	pavement or footpath
raincoat		mackintosh
trunk (of a car)		boot

Prefixes and Suffixes

Note to Home Read this page with your student. Use it as a reference for identifying words that have prefixes and suffixes in books you read together.

Prefixes

A **prefix** can be at the beginning of a word.

Prefix	Meaning	Example Word
un-	not; opposite	unkind = not kind
		untie = the opposite of tie
re-	again	reread = to read again

Can you help me *untie* my shoelaces?

Suffixes

A **suffix** can be at the end of a word.

Suffix	Meaning	Example Word
-er	one who	painter = one who paints
-ful	full of	joyful = full of joy

The pretty music makes me feel *joyful.*

Base Words

Note to Home Read this page with your student. Help him or her identify the prefixes or suffixes in the second list below (*-er, -ing, un-, -s, re-, -ed, -ness, -ly*). Extend learning by helping your student identify base words in books you read together.

A **base word** is a word without a prefix or suffix.

Base Words

teach	read	bright
like	climb	slow

Words With Prefixes or Suffixes

teacher	*unlike*	*reread*	*brightness*
teaching	*likes*	*climbed*	*slowly*

Dolch Words

Note to Home The words in this list are from the core word list known as the Dolch 220 Basic Sight Vocabulary. They also appear in the vocabulary lessons in this book. Periodically quiz your student on his or her ability to recognize and read these sight words.

The **Dolch Words** are basic words every reader should learn.

after	every	let	pretty	under
again	fall	like	pull	up
all	fast	little	read	use
ask	find	long	ride	very
away	from	look	right	walk
because	full	make	round	want
before	funny	never	run	warm
best	give	new	say	wash
big	good	now	see	we
bring	help	off	sleep	well
by	hold	old	small	what
call	hot	on	soon	when
can	how	once	start	where
carry	if	one	stop	which
cold	into	open	take	who
cut	jump	our	tell	why
down	keep	out	to	wish
draw	kind	over	today	with
drink	know	pick	together	work
eat	laugh	play	try	write

Fun With Words

Note to Home Read this page with your student. Ask him or her to identify objects or animals that match each sound word. Then help your student identify the two words in each compound word.

Sound Words

A **sound word** is a word that sounds like what it means.

Sound Words			
buzz	ring	boom	cluck
clap	purr	moo	hiss

Compound Words

A **compound word** is one word that is made of two words.

Compound Words	
basketball	lifeguard
birdhouse	pancake
doorbell	seashell
grandmother	snowman

Dictionary Skills

Note to Home If you have a picture dictionary, refer to it as you read this page with your student. Help your student look up his or her favorite words.

A **dictionary** is a book that lists words and their meanings. Some dictionaries have pictures to show you what the words mean.

beehive

desk

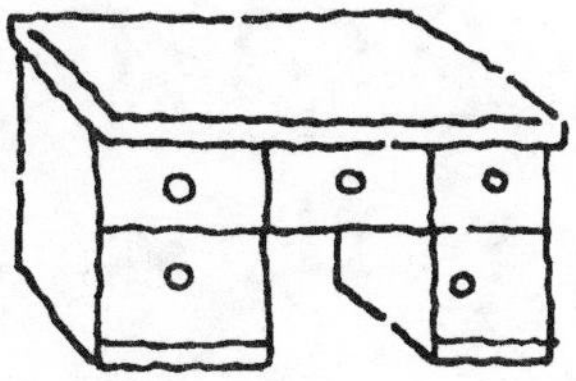

stump

A dictionary may also show the word in a sentence.

He got honey from the **beehive.**

I keep pencils in my **desk.**

The frog sat on the **stump.**

Dictionary Skills

Note to Home Read this page with your student. Quiz him or her on alphabetical order by using the vocabulary words in this book. For example, "Which word comes first in the dictionary—*glue* or *artist?*"

ABC Order

The words in a dictionary are in ABC order. This is also called alphabetical order.

A B C D E F G H I J K L M N
O P Q R S T U V W X Y Z
a b c d e f g h i j k l m n
o p q r s t u v w x y z

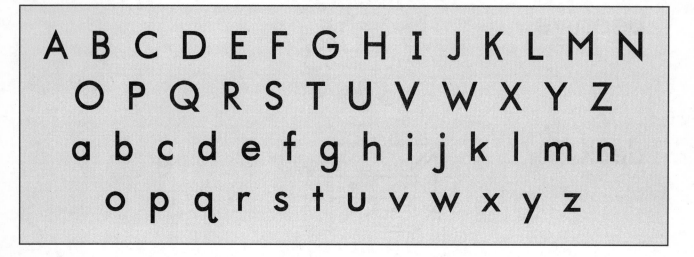

To find a word in a dictionary, you need to know its beginning letter.

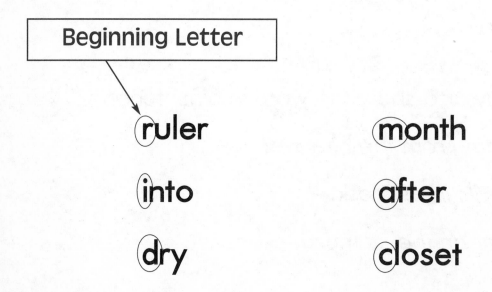

Beginning Letter

ruler	month
into	after
dry	closet

Nouns, Verbs, and Adjectives

Note to Home Read this page with your student to introduce parts of speech. Choose a book that contains simple sentences, and lead your student in identifying nouns, verbs, and adjectives.

Nouns

A **noun** names things, people, animals, or places.

Nouns			
book	library	teacher	goldfish
nail	post office	student	firefly

Verbs

A **verb** shows an action or tells what something or someone is or has.

Verbs			
read	is	has	eat
jump	own	see	drink

Adjectives

An **adjective** tells more about a noun.

Adjectives			
funny	strong	good	soft

My **funny** *friend makes me laugh.*

A **strong** *wind rattled the windows.*

Note to Home The glossary provides a meaningful context for each vocabulary word presented in this book. Use it as a reference to reinforce your student's understanding of the vocabulary words.

Glossary

A a

aboard We went **aboard** the ship.

address My street **address** is 321 Oak Lane.

afraid I am not **afraid** of the dark.

after Brush your teeth **after** you eat.

afternoon In the **afternoon,** the sun is shining.

again Let's sing that song **again.**

age Your **age** is how old you are.

air Kick the ball up in the **air.**

all **All** eight of us were on the bus.

American A person from The United States is called an **American.**

ant That tiny black insect is an **ant.**

anthill An **anthill** covers a nest of ants.

appear Stars **appear** at night.

artist The **artist** drew a picture of her cat.

ask **Ask** the teacher for help.

aunt My **aunt** is my mother's sister.

autumn **Autumn** comes between summer and winter.

away **1.** The cat ran **away** from us.
2. How far **away** is the park?

B b

backyard We have a fence around the **backyard.**

ball **1.** A **ball** is round. **2.** Cinderella danced at the **ball.**

bang **1.** I can **bang** the drums. **2.** The door closed with a **bang.**

bank Put your money in the **bank.**

bare **1.** We walk on the sand in our **bare** feet. **2.** The shelf was **bare**; there was nothing on it.

bathroom I wash in the **bathroom.**

bay A **bay** is a small part of a sea or lake.

beach That **beach** has white sand.

bear A **bear** can catch a fish with one paw.

because Sam likes frogs **because** they jump.

bed I sleep in my own **bed.**

beehive He got honey from the **beehive.**

before **1.** I brush my teeth **before** I go to bed. **2.** She was **before,** or in front of, me in line.

behind The second person in line is **behind** the first person.

best She is the **best** reader in the class.

between **1.** The peanut butter is **between** the slices of bread. **2.** I take a nap **between** three and four o'clock.

big Tigers are very **big** cats.

birdbath The bird splashed in the **birdbath.**

birdhouse A bird flew into the **birdhouse** to get some seeds.

bloom When flowers **bloom,** they show their brightly colored petals.

blow Watch me **blow** out the candles.

blustery The **blustery** wind blew the leaves around.

boat A **boat** is smaller than a ship.

book Which **book** should I read?

bounce A rubber ball can **bounce** high into the air.

brave Firefighters are **brave.**

breeze A **breeze** is a soft wind.

brick A **brick** is a block of clay used for building.

bright The sun is **bright** today.

bring Do you **bring** your lunch to school?

build You can **build** a house with wood.

bulldog A **bulldog** is a kind of dog that has short legs.

bulletin board Post your drawing on the **bulletin board.**

bumpy The car bounced on the **bumpy** road.

bus stop I wait for the bus at the **bus stop.**

buzz **1.** Bees **buzz** around pretty flowers. **2.** I hear the **buzz** of a fly.

C c

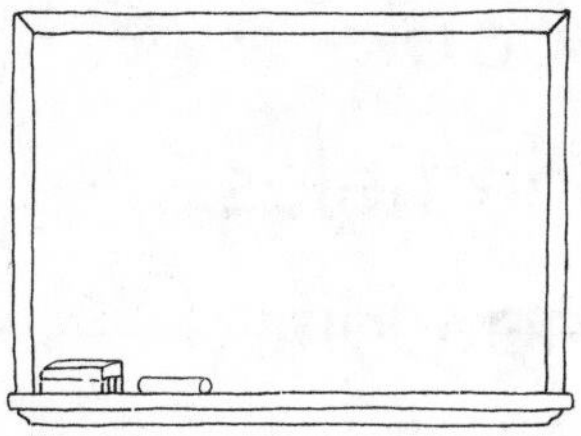

call **1.** My dog comes to me when I **call.** **2.** We **call** our dog Clifford. **3.** I **call** my grandparents on the telephone.

can **1.** You **can** swim fast. **2.** Please open this **can** of soup.

care People show that they **care** by being kind.

carry It is smart to **carry** an umbrella on a cloudy day.

cashier We pay the **cashier** at the store.

catfish A **catfish** is a fish that has whiskers.

chair Goldilocks sat on the **chair.**

ABC

chalkboard Our teacher uses chalk to write on the **chalkboard.**

clap **Clap** your hands one time.

classroom The **classroom** has ten desks.

climb A spider can **climb** up a wall.

close Please **close** the door when you leave.

closet Hang your coat in the **closet.**

cold Ice makes drinks **cold.**

color **1.** The **color** of grass is green.
2. Use a crayon to **color** this picture.

cool The weather is **cool** in the fall.

copy **1. Copy** me by doing what I do.
2. There is one **copy** of this book.

corn **Corn** is a grain that grows in fields.

country Our **country** is called The United States of America.

cowbell The **cowbell** around the cow's neck is ringing.

crayon There is a red **crayon** in the box.

curb Wait at the **curb** for the crosswalk sign to change.

cut The teacher **cut** the paper in half.

D d

dark **Dark** means not bright.

date Today's **date** is August 10.

deep Snakes dig **deep** holes into the earth.

dentist The **dentist** looks at my teeth.

desk I keep pencils in my **desk.**

dinner We eat **dinner** at six o'clock.

disappear The sun seems to **disappear** at night.

doctor A **doctor** helps sick people.

door She opened the **door** when I knocked.

down A seesaw goes up and **down.**

draw You can **draw** a picture with a pencil.

drink **1.** Mom's favorite **drink** is tea.
2. I **drink** milk with my lunch.

drive Mary can **drive** you home in her new car.

dry **Dry** means not wet at all.

E e

earth **1.** We planted seeds in the **earth.**
2. We live on **Earth.**

eat I **eat** eggs for breakfast.

everyone **Everyone** can play this game.

F f

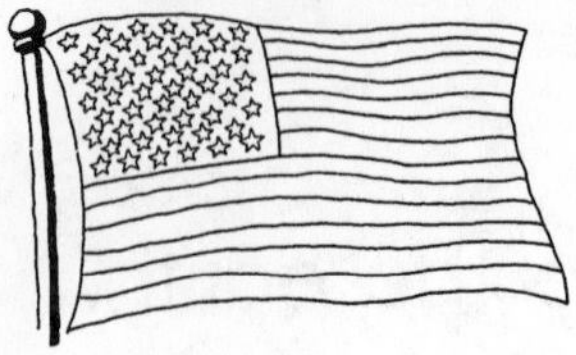

fall **1.** Autumn is the same as **fall.**
2. Leaves **fall** from trees.

farmer The **farmer** has two cows.

fast A rabbit can run **fast.**

find Help me **find** my hat.

firefly A **firefly** is an insect that glows.

firehouse The fire truck goes to the **firehouse.**

fireplace We use our **fireplace** in winter.

fit Does the piece **fit** into the puzzle?

fix She will **fix** my broken toy.

flag Our **flag** is red, white, and blue.

floor **1.** We walk on the **floor.**
2. The school has two **floors.**

flour We need **flour** to bake a cake.

flower He picked a red **flower** from his garden.

follow **1.** My dogs **follow** me around the backyard. **2.** Spring **follows** winter.

from **1.** The present is **from** my sister.
2. The train leaves **from** the station.
3. Two **from** five leaves three.

fruit Apples are my favorite **fruit.**

full **1.** The pool is **full** of water.
2. I have a **full** stomach after lunch.

funny I like **funny** jokes.

G g

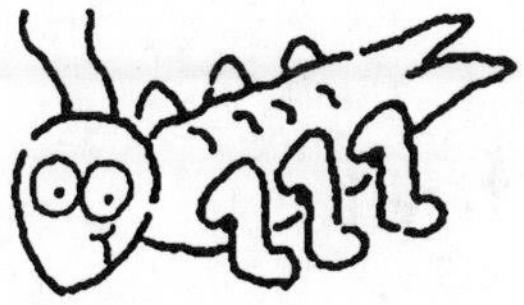

game That **game** was fun!

garden She grows flowers in her **garden.**

give I **give** a card to my grandmother.

glue We need **glue** to fix the toy.

goal **1.** My **goal** is to read well.
2. Kick the ball into the **goal.**

goldfish The **goldfish** swims around and around.

good **1.** The **good** boy shared his toys.
2. I like to eat **good** food. **3.** The dogs were **good** and did not bark.

grass My father cut the **grass** today.

grasshopper A **grasshopper** is an insect that hops.

group A **group** is more than two.

gust A strong **gust** of wind knocked over the flowerpot.

H h

hair Her **hair** is very long and dark.

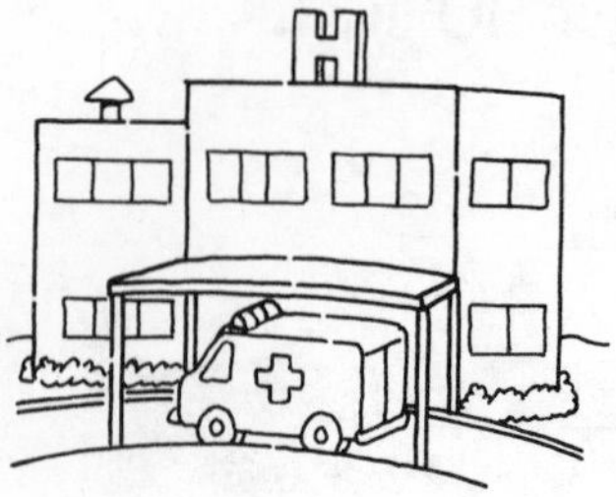

half **1.** One is **half** of two. **2.** The glass is **half** full.

hammer **1.** She used a **hammer** to build the table. **2.** He can **hammer** the nail.

hang Spiders **hang** in their webs.

happy **1.** We are **happy** in our new house. **2.** I had a **happy** birthday.

hard **1.** The **hard** rocks hurt our feet. **2.** Work **hard** and do your best.

hare A **hare** looks like a rabbit.

headlight My bike's **headlight** is bright.

hear I **hear** a bird singing.

help I **help** my mother clean the house.

hold **Hold** my hand to cross the street.

honk **1.** The cars' horns **honk.** **2.** The **honk** of the horn was loud.

hood The car's engine is under the **hood.**

hop Rabbits **hop** from place to place.

hospital My doctor works in a **hospital.**

hot **1.** The stove in the kitchen is **hot.** **2.** I do not like **hot** weather.

how **How** do you say this word?

I i

idea I have an **idea** for a new game.

if I will swing **if** I go to the park.

insect A fly is a kind of **insect.**

into **1.** Run **into** the house if it rains.
2. I fell **into** the puddle of water.

J j

join We **join** my aunt for dinner.

jump How high can you **jump?**

K k

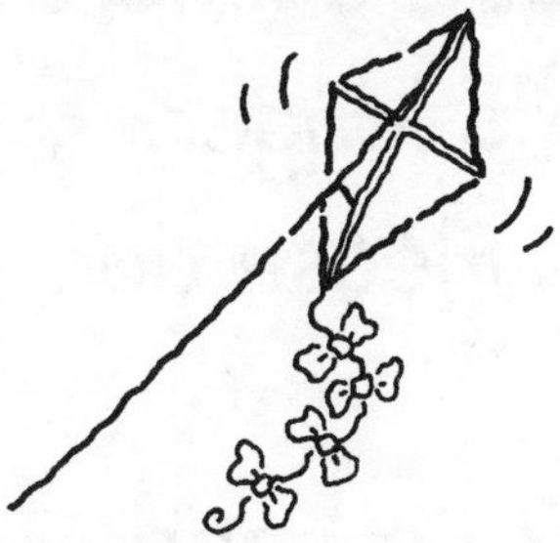

keep **1.** I wear a hat to **keep** my head warm. **2.** Can you **keep** a secret?

kind **1.** Always be **kind** to animals.
2. I like this **kind** of snack.

kitchen We eat lunch in the **kitchen.**

kite Her **kite** was high in the sky.

know I **know** how to play ball.

L l

land The **land** is under your feet.

laugh **1.** I **laugh** when I am happy.
2. He has a funny **laugh.**

lazy He is too **lazy** and will not help.

leader A **leader** shows the way.

leaf **1.** A **leaf** fell off the tree. **2.** The **leaves** turn red in the fall.

learn I will **learn** how to dance.

let Please **let** me have a crayon.

library The **library** has many books.

license You need a **license** to drive a car.

lift Don't **lift** that heavy box.

like **1.** Dogs **like** treats. **2.** He was dressed **like** a clown.

listen We **listen** to the birds sing.

little **1.** The baby is **little.** **2.** That is a **little** ladybug. **3.** Please wait a **little** longer.

long **1.** Her hair is very **long.** **2.** Please do not stay **long** at the park.

look **1. Look** at this book. **2.** Take a good **look** at this bug.

lunch We eat **lunch** at school.

M m

make A bird can **make** a nest.

mark **Mark** this date on the calendar.

market We go to the **market** to buy food.

month **1.** May is a **month.** **2.** There are twelve **months** in a year.

morning **Morning** is the first part of the day.

museum There is a lot of art in the **museum.**

N n

nail A **nail** holds pieces of wood together.

never I have **never** told a lie.

new He bought **new** socks because the old ones had holes.

night The moon comes out at **night.**

now She was at the house, but she is at school **now.**

nurse The **nurse** took my temperature.

nut A peanut is a kind of **nut.**

O o

off Turn **off** the stove when you are finished cooking.

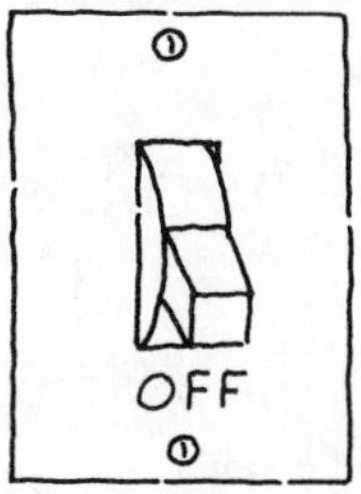
OFF

old I got a new bike because my **old** one broke.

on I put a hat **on** my head.

once **Once** means one time.

open May I **open** a window?

our **Our** room is neat and clean.

out We went **out** to play.

over The frog jumped **over** the hole.

own Soon I will have my **own** desk.

P p

POST OFFICE
MAIL

paint **1.** My goal is to **paint** pretty pictures.
2. This can of **paint** is new.

park The **park** has flowers and grass.

pedal **1.** I **pedal** my bike hard.
2. The **pedals** on a bike make it go.

pencil My **pencil** is yellow.

pick We **pick** flowers from our garden.

picture She drew a **picture** of a funny ape.

plan **1.** I **plan** to read three books by December. **2.** I have a **plan** to solve the problem.

play **1.** May we **play** at your house today? **2.** I like to **play** the piano. **3.** The actors in the **play** were funny.

pond We saw a frog in the **pond.**

poster I had to hang a **poster** on the wall.

post office A **post office** sends mail.

president A **president** is the leader of a country.

pretty She looked **pretty** in her dress.

pull A horse can **pull** a wagon.

push I can **push** the swing.

Q q

quiet The library is **quiet.**

R r

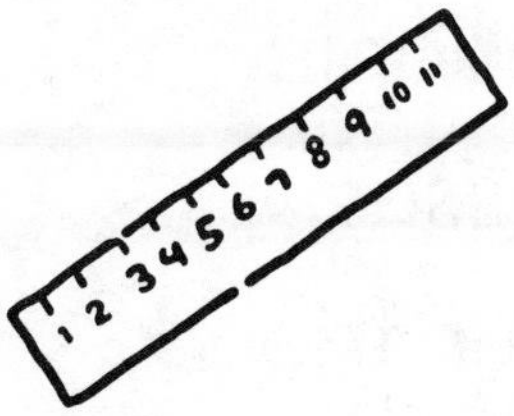

race **1.** Which team won the **race?**
2. I can **race** you down the street.

rattle **1.** Give the baby her **rattle.**
2. The wind **rattles** the windows.

reach Can you **reach** the top shelf?

read I like to **read** books.

restaurant A **restaurant** is a place where you can eat dinner.

ride **1.** He likes to **ride** horses. **2.** We took a **ride** in the car.

right **1.** Which hand is your **right?**
2. I thought I was **right,** but I was wrong.

rock A **rock** is a hard piece of earth.

room **1.** Is there **room** for me to sit here?
2. Our house has seven **rooms.**

round An orange is **round.**

ruler A **ruler** measures things.

run I like to **run** in races.

S s

sad He was **sad** when his dog ran away.

sail **1.** The boat had a big, white **sail.** **2.** The boat will **sail** out to sea.

say To **say** is to speak.

scare Dark rooms **scare** some people.

see I cannot **see** without my glasses.

share We **share** our toys with our friends.

shell **1.** I found a pretty **shell** on the beach. **2.** A turtle has a **shell.**

ship A **ship** is a very large boat.

shore A **shore** is land by an ocean or a lake.

short His hair is cut very **short.**

sidewalk Walk on the **sidewalk** instead of the street.

sign A **sign** tells you about important things.

sled A **sled** helps people move through snow.

sleep It is important to **sleep** at night.

slide **1.** You can **slide** down this hill. **2.** The **slide** on the playground is tall and fast.

slow **1.** A turtle is a **slow** animal. **2. Slow** down when the light turns yellow.

small Goldfish are **small** fish.

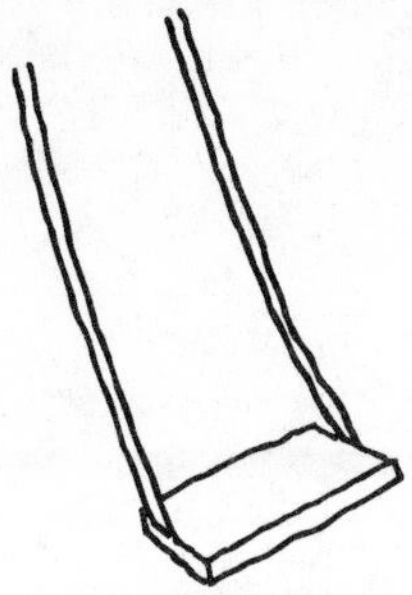

smooth The frozen pond is very **smooth.**

snow **Snow** falls in the winter.

soft A pillow is **soft.**

son A boy baby is called a **son.**

soon The bus will be here **soon.**

spring **Spring** is between winter and summer.

start The movie will **start** at two o'clock.

state Florida is a **state** in America.

stop **1.** I watched the car **stop** in the street. **2.** Where is the **stop** to get on the bus?

storm A **storm** brings wind and rain.

strong The **strong** wind knocked over the tree.

student A **student** learns at a school.

summer **Summer** is between spring and fall.

sun The **sun** gives us light and heat.

swing **1.** Can you push me in the **swing?** **2.** I can **swing** high in the air.

T t

take We need to **take** the books to the library.

tall Giraffes are **tall** animals.

teacher A **teacher** helps you learn.

tell **Tell** me a story.

think You use your brain to **think.**

tight Tie a **tight** knot.

to My father drives me **to** school in the morning.

today **Today** is the day right now.

together We can play **together.**

tomorrow **Tomorrow** is the day after today.

tools **Tools** help us make things.

tree A **tree** has branches and leaves.

trunk **1.** A **trunk** is in the back of a car. **2.** We keep our winter sweaters in a **trunk.** **3.** The elephant picked up a peanut with his **trunk.**

try Always **try** to do your best.

U u

under My ruler was **under** my book.

United States The **United States** is a country.

up Climb **up** to the top of the hill.

use We **use** glue to make pictures in school.

V v

vegetable A carrot is a **vegetable.**

very I am **very** sorry.

W w

wait We had to **wait** at the doctor's office.

wake I **wake** up at six o'clock to go to school.

walk **1.** We **walk** to school. **2.** We went for a **walk** in the park.

want I **want** to go home now.

warm The sun is **warm** on a spring day.

wash We **wash** our hands before a meal.

we **We** went on a family trip.

week There are seven days in one **week.**

weekend We do not go to school on the **weekend.**

well I am **well.** How are you?

wet The grass is **wet** from the rain.

what **What** do you think of that?

when **When** is winter?

where **Where** is your hat?

which **Which** bus is the right one?

whistle **1.** Can you **whistle** a song? **2.** Blow the **whistle** at the end of the game.

who **Who** can play this game?

why **Why** is the sky blue?

win We want to **win** the game.

windmill A **windmill** uses wind to make energy.

window We looked out the **window** to see the snow.

windshield The wipers cleaned the rain off the **windshield.**

winter **Winter** comes between fall and spring.

wish **1.** You may have any fish you **wish.**
2. Did you make a birthday **wish?**

with Take your book **with** you.

work Farmers **work** on farms.

write I **write** letters to my grandmother.

Y y

year **1.** There are 365 days in a **year.**
2. I am five **years** old today.

yesterday **Yesterday** is the day before today.

young Kittens are **young** cats.

A–F Word Bank

G—M Word Bank

N—S Word Bank

T–Z Word Bank